Better Bikes!

A MANUAL FOR EXPANDED USE OF BICYCLES

Tom Cuthbertson

ILLUSTRATED BY KAREN LUSEBRINK

Ten Speed Press

1♻

BETTER BIKES!
is published by Ten Speed Press, Box 7123, Berkeley, California 94707.

© Copyright 1980 by Tom Cuthbertson

ISBN 0-89815-024-8 paper
ISBN 0-89815-025-6 cloth

Beverly Anderson Graphic Design, type set by Type & Graphics
Printed in The United States of America
by Consolidated Printers, Inc.

Contents

Introduction

THE BICYCLE is the most efficient form of transportation on earth. But bikes are often a pain in the rear. Cycling is the highest natural high of all, but it takes only one sharp tack to deflate the whole experience.

This book is about setting up and using bicycles to get the most out of them. I have taken a very close look at the basic ten-speed and several alternative bikes I use myself, and covered all the special things you can fix up on machines like these so you can do almost all your short work and recreation trips by bicycle.

For people who already enjoy cycling in one way or another, there are detailed instructions on how to deal with the myriad problems the cyclist encounters, from the good old flat tire to the knotty question of how to deal with vehicular traffic.

All these ideas assume that you already ride a bike a good deal. For those of you who don't ride much, even though you know how and have a bike stuck back in the garage somewhere, the first thing you have to do is take a special bike joyride, just to see what the whole experience is about. No matter how efficient a bike is in comparison to a gas-gulping, smog-belching car, the bike can do nothing if you don't take it out of the garage and leave the car behind for a change.

So the next time you have an hour or so on a warm, pleasant day, take a short ride and introduce yourself, or get a reintroduction, to the joy of cycling. Plan a little before you take the ride, so it will be as comfortable, easy, and hassle-free as possible. Choose a bike that you know will be fun for *you* to ride. That doesn't necessarily mean a shiny racing bike. You may be more at ease on a sit-down bike with coaster brakes and a cushy seat. If so, fine. Get whatever bike you like best for your introduction-to-joy-ride. Just try to get a light one so you don't have to work too hard to get it going. Get a bike that's in good working order, too. Have a good mechanic check it over if you aren't used to working on bikes yourself. The brakes and gears should work well, and the tires should be in good shape and inflated to the proper pressure.

Pick a quiet, fairly level area for your introductory ride. On weekend mornings there are many residential areas or paved paths along the shores of lakes, rivers, and beaches that are perfect. Take a quiet, unhurried ride in your chosen area, and tune in to your senses. Feel how nice it is to have your feet going around in those smooth, almost effortless circles.

If you come to a steep little hill, don't fight it. Get off and walk rather than trying to ride up. When you coast downhill, keep the speed reasonable, but feel the wind, sniff the air, take a deep breath of it, and let it out slowly. Yeah, you'll start to get the hang of it, real quick.

All you have to do is look, smell, listen, and FEEL a little. It's such basic stuff, we all tend to forget it. Especially if we spend much of our time cooped up in houses, offices, and cars all day. But once you get back in touch with the simple joys of a pleasant ride outdoors, once you get in tune with the delight of moving so easily, so gracefully under your *own* power on a bicycle, you'll want to do it more and more.

To keep you riding right, so your first joyride can be followed by a long and growing relationship with bikes, choose a bike that fits your needs and your tastes. Then use the appropriate parts of this book to fix it up and care for it so you aren't put off by any of the hassles that can make cycling lose its appeal.

If you're prepared for the lumps and bumps and know how to deal with them, you can almost always prevail on a bike. That's what grows on you. You do it yourself. You get this feeling that no matter what OPEC, the government, and all the forces of labor and big business do, you can still get from point A to point B, all by yourself. And you have a good time while you're at it!

Part I
The Ten-Speed Revisited

Chapter 1
Getting into Gear Again

IF YOU HAVE a ten-speed but you don't ride it much, use this chapter to find out why you aren't riding the bike and what you can do to get rolling again. You're probably hung up in one of three ways: either the bike isn't working right, or it works OK but just isn't set up right for your needs, or it works great, but *you* can't get up the gumption to start riding it regularly.

The best source of gumption is joy. Read the introduction to the book, take a joyride, then see the appropriate chapters if you need help to get into commuting, running errands, or taking long trips on your newfound joyride machine.

If you're up for cycling but your bike refuses to work, take the bike to a good mechanic or use one of the good repair manuals like *Anybody's Bike Book, Glenn's Complete Bicycle Manual,* or *Richard's Bicycle Book* to help you get the bike in A-1 shape. If you can't find those books in your area, order one from any of the catalogues listed in the Addresses section at the back of this book.

If both you and your bike are working OK, but you still do most of your short trips around town in a gas-gulping automobile, just ask yourself, "What's keeping me from riding that bike?"

Is it that the bike seems sluggish, uncomfortable, and hard to pedal compared to other bikes? This could be because it's overweight (bikes are that way almost as often as people), or because it has a seat that gives you a royal pain, or because you can't carry things on it without dropping them, or because little details like soft tires and a squeaky chain make cycling slow, troublesome, and inefficient. See Chapter 2 and fix up your bike so that it not only works, but works as EFFICIENTLY as

1

possible. The bicycle can be the most efficient means of transportation on earth; if you can accept and enjoy its pace, you can quickly learn how to keep it at its peak of efficiency, adapting it to your every need.

Are you afraid to ride around town in the traffic? I don't blame you. You seem to be at such a disadvantage, riding a 20- or 30-lb bike in a world dominated by 2-ton growling smudge-pots. But cycling can be as safe as or safer than using a car. If you avoid busy streets, learn a few basic self-defense tricks to use when you can't avoid the traffic, and wear a helmet, your odds for serious injury are reduced to almost nothing. And you'll find that the safety-oriented approach outlined in Chapter 3 is a refreshing change from all the rat-racing you have to do to drive a car through traffic snarls, park it in crowded parking lots, and fill it with dwindling fuel supplies.

Are you fed up with flats? Some ten-speeds seem to get many more flat tires than others, and some riding situations call for special equipment and/or techniques to avoid popping and/or leaky tires. To rid yourself of this major biking bugaboo, see Chapter 4, Solving the Flat Problem.

Has your ten-speed been ripped off? Or are you terrified that it will get ripped off? I lost my beloved bike to a thief once, and I got so depressed I felt like giving up cycling forever. But I got over it and pinched and saved and rode clunkers until I could get a nice new bike, which in fact turned out to be vastly superior to the old one. I worried terribly about losing my shiny new Hetchins at first, but it got a lot less shiny after a while, and became the same sort of old-shoe companion my first bike had been. I also learned how and when and where to lock it, so I don't worry much any more. It's crazy to have a wonderful bicycle and not use it precisely because you think it's so wonderful that it'll be snatched. See Chapter 5 for a whole new approach to bike security, emphasizing the practical instead of the paranoiac.

Do you have hassles when you try to carry things on your ten-speed? Bikes with the racy high-seat, dropped-handlebar configuration aren't set up well for carrying the week's groceries. I mean, whoever heard of a Tour de France champion with a dozen eggs, a bottle of wine, or even one of those aerodynamic skinny loaves of French bread strapped to the bike? There are several different ways to carry stuff on a ten-speed. Some are simple, but others take some time and money in order to prepare the vehicle for bigger loads. Depending on the size of your household and your preferences for bike use, you can find a method that fits your needs. Once you've got the bike set up according to the plan in Chapter 6 that suits you, use the techniques covered in that same chapter to do all your normal shopping with ease and convenience. For carrying exceptionally large loads, alternative bikes such as the three-speed "station wagon" or the bike-and-trailer rig covered in Chapter 10 may be what you need.

Have you had daydreams of taking a long vacation bike ride through the open countryside? But do these dreams seem more like nightmares when you look at the bedraggled cycle-tourists you meet on the road? Touring on a bike *is* hard work, but you can minimize the work and maximize the fun if you read Chapter 7 and learn how to plan and prepare for a long bike trip.

Do you shut your bike up in the closet the minute the first rain, frost, or snow appears in the fall? Shame on you! There's a way to get along on a bike in rough weather, and it is described in Chapter 8. It isn't the most pleasant sort of cycling, but if you are well-prepared for the elements, you can ride an any but the worst stormy weather.

The chapters in Part II of this book cover bicycle alternatives that fill the needs your good old ten-speed just can't fill. If all the fooling and fiddling you do by using the first half of the book doesn't bring your ten-speed up to the tasks you have in mind for it, go on into that second part and find out which bike you need, be it anything from a kid's Moto-X racer to a super-light long-distance road machine.

Chapter 2
Make Your Ten-Speed More Efficient

TEN-SPEEDS aren't always ten times faster than other bikes. If you have a heavy and rough-running ten-speed, it may actually be slower than a light and efficient one-speed. So if your ten-speed is sluggish or uncomfortable, check each of the following sections for problems and fix up what needs fixing. The items are listed with the easiest to fix first, and if you take care of the tires and chain, the first two items, chances are your bike will be noticeably better; keep this in mind whenever you sense the bike is a little slower than it should be; a quick dose of air in the tires and oil on the chain may be all you need.

Tires

Do the tires feel soft? Pump them up to the pressure that's recommended on the sidewall. Standard tires call for a pump with a little thumbblock lever on the attaching end; the pumps that have screw-on ends (or "chucks" as they are called) have a nasty habit of letting all the pressure out of your tire as you unscrew the chuck. For tires with the spiffy Presta valves (the skinny kind with the tiny cap that screws down tight) you have to loosen the tiny cap, push it in for a sec to make sure it's loose, then press on either a chuck of a frame pump (the kind that fits on the bike frame) or an adapter chuck that you can use with the thumbblock end on your standard pump. See Illustration 13 to find out which pump set-up you need.

Even if you don't know the recommended pressure for your tires, and even if you don't have a pressure gauge, you can still check for the proper inflation of each tire before you go for a ride. Put one of the wheels down on the edge of a curb or stair as in Illustration 1 and lean your upper body over the handlebars or seat so you can shove down sharply. Watch for the little flare of the tire as the edge of the stair or curb squishes into it. If that edge doesn't squish into the tire at all each time you shove down, the tire is too hard. It may pop when you go over a rock or chuckhole. If the edge squishes all the way through the tire, and you feel the rim clunk as it "bottoms out" each time you push down hard, then the tire is too soft. Let out air or pump in air until the tire pressure is right. It's right when you see the tire bulge just a bit at the edge of the curb or stair each time you shove down.

Maybe your tires are slow and clunky even when they are pumped up right. How fat are they? How thick is the rubber on the sidewalls? The wider the cross section of a tire, the more of it pushes against the ground as it rolls along. The thicker the sidewalls, the heavier and "cushier" the tire will be. A fat tire gives you lots of shock-absorbing cushion against bumps and pebbles, but it makes for much more rolling resistance. It feels like you're riding on a flat tire, even when it's full of air. What's worse, if a fat tire gets worn down so the tread is thin where it hits the ground, it will be *more* susceptible to punctures than a narrow tire with thick tread at the point of contact. For this

Illustration **1**   Checking Tire Pressure

reason, most fat tires are extra thick all the way around, making them outrageously overweight. And all that weight has to whirl around and around while you are riding the bike, soaking up your energy like a flywheel, making it harder to accelerate *and* slow down. *BAH!*

If your tires are so heavy it's hard for you to get them spinning, go to a good tourist/racing-type bike shop or get a good catalogue (see Addresses) and buy tires that are as narrow

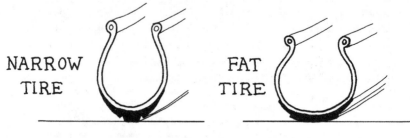

NARROW
TIRE

FAT
TIRE

Illustration **2**   Tire Profiles

and light as possible for your rim size. If your rims are made to take 27-by-1¼-inch tires, for instance, you can get tires that are less than an inch wide. Some of these modern narrow-profile tires are stronger and longer-lasting than others; the Specialized Bicycle Imports Touring tire sets a high standard with its long-lasting center ridge of rubber, its strong double casing of nylon, and its fine handling characteristics. Other narrow and light tires by Specialized Bicycle Imports, National, IRC, and other companies can be good too; for further info on them, see Chapter 4, page 34. If you have sew-ups and are bothered more by flats than by sluggishness of the tires, see Chapter 4 for info on converting to the modern narrow-light standard-clincher tires, which can feel almost as nice as sew-ups, without all the hassles.

Chain

You can perk up the performance of your ten-speed by simply oiling its dry and squeaky chain. You'll be amazed at the difference a nice smooth-flowing, easy-shifting chain makes. Use a light-to-medium-weight (10W to 20W) motor oil or cycle oil and let it dribble onto the chain as you slowly turn the pedals backward. Make sure the gear changer is set accurately in a gear, so

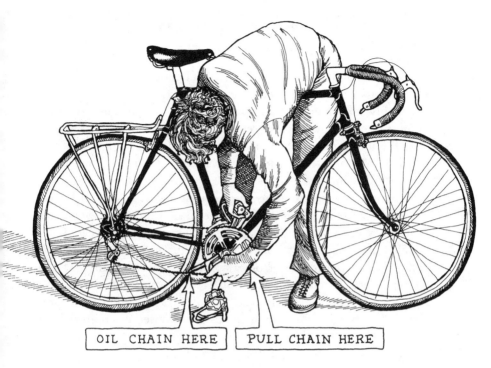

OIL CHAIN HERE   PULL CHAIN HERE

Illustration **3**   Caring for Chain

the chain will run easily without skipping or jamming. If the chain is gunky and dirty, rinse it out with a very light oil or a penetrating lubricant like LPS1. Put a lot of it on the chain, run the pedal backward for twenty revolutions or so to work the stuff in and loosen up the gunk. Then take a rag, soak it lightly with the thin oil, and wipe the chain off, turning the pedals a bit now and then so you can rub the chain between the front and rear sprockets and get all of it clean. If there is loads of gunk on the chain, you may need to run a little brush (a coffee percolator brush works perfectly, but don't ever use yours in the percolator after cleaning a chain with it!) to whisk out the gunk between the link sideplates. When the chain is clean, apply heavier oil for lasting lubrication. Light stuff like LPS1 or WD40 or sewing machine oil may look real slick, but it doesn't last long enough to be practical, especially in wet weather.

When your chain is lubed, check to make sure it isn't stretched out too much. Pinch the links between your fingers (blech!) at the point shown in Illustration 3 and pull the chain forward. If it slacks off the chainwheel enough that you can see the points of the sprocket under it, you need a new chain and probably a new set of rear sprockets to get your ten-speed running smoothly. See a good repair manual or a good bike shop to get the job done properly; it's a tough and messy operation, but well worth the effort when you can zoom around with a silent, smooth-flowing chain.

While we're thinking about that messy chain, are you bugged by the fact that your pants cuff on your right leg always turns a greasy black after you've ridden your ten-speed for a while? You can either roll that cuff up, or use an elastic cuff band to keep the cuff from flapping against the dirty works down there. Good shops and better catalogues (see Addresses) carry cuff bands with velcro stuff that sticks together when you wrap the band tight. Some bands have reflective material on them; this can really add to your visibility at night, so get the reflective type of cuff band if you can find it.

Seat

If your rear end or your crotch is so uncomfortable when you cycle that you can't think of anything else, don't torture yourself; get a better seat! Even if you have to spend almost as much on the seat as you did on the bike (some secondhand bikes cost *less* than some fancy new seats), a comfortable bike seat is worth every penny. There are now different options, ranging from racy-looking thin saddles with little built-in lumps of padding, to medium-width plastic seats with a layer of padding over the top, to wide leather saddles with springs that are great for sit-down-style bikes. And there are always the classic leather racing and touring saddles, which most people find hard and painful at first, but which break in and fit you better than any other seat if you can stick with them. For detailed information on all the types, see pages 74, 92, 131.

Whatever seat you try, get it attached to the seatpost properly, with a strong mounting bracket that fits both the seat rails and the end of the post EXACTLY. Otherwise, the thing will come loose and flop around so you can never stay comfortable on it. Set the seat at such a height that you can straighten your leg when each foot (held flat-footed) is at the bottom of the pedal revolution. Tip the seat back and forth while the clamp is still loose, and set it either level, or with the nose tipped up just a little, depending on which is more comfortable. Then tighten the nuts on both sides of the seat clamp, each a little at a time, so you lock the seat in position completely, with no chance of its working loose and slopping up and down. If it *does* slop up and down like that, it will quickly ruin the toothed surfaces on the clamp that are supposed to hold the seat still. In this case, you'll have to get a new clamp and start over.

If you can't feel comfortable on a narrow ten-speed seat no matter how you set it, and then find that if you switch to a wider seat you just chafe and rub your thighs while trying to ride in the racy ten-speed position, maybe you should consider converting your bike to the slow but stable upright riding position, as described in Chapter 6. This requires that you get a sit-down-type seat, like those in Illustration 26. But with a good seat you can take fairly long rides without soreness of the fanny, and although you may not be as fast as those bent-over racers, you'll get there feeling a lot better.

Brakes

Brakes shouldn't slow you down unless you apply them. When you take your hand off the brake handle, the thing should let go of the rim of the wheel, completely. If your brakes drag or are slow to release, you have to do a little diagnostic trip to find out just where the problem is, then you can fix it. *Anybody's Bike Book* has a very good section on the subject, I'm proud to say. If you don't want to fix the brakes yourself, let a good shop do the job. If your rear brake is on all the time because you have a rack back there that has come loose and mashed down on the brake mechanism, see the section on the special rack support that's down a few paragraphs. Once the rack is held up securely, it won't make your brakes drag anymore.

If your brakes DON'T work well enough when you apply them, especially when the wheels are wet, you can now take care of the problem with a modernized set of brake pads. I have never had any trouble stopping with stock pads, as long as I have remembered to apply my wet brakes gently *before* I needed them. This has always whisked enough of the water off so that I have been able to stop OK. But you may have more trouble with your brakes when they get wet. If you do, try some of those fancy high-priced Matthauser or Kool Stop brake pads, or some of the cheaper models, such as the new Weinman X-pattern brake pads. Any of these pads will give you vastly improved brake power in adverse conditions. If you want to go all the way, and get brakes that will stop at ANYTHING, you can have posts brazed onto your forks and seat stays and install the kind of cantilever brakes they use on tandem bikes and cyclo-cross racing machines. If you have strong hands and big Mafac cantilever brakes, you can always put enough if not more than enough braking friction on your wheels. The limiting factor then becomes the traction of the wheels and the ground. To me it seems more important to practice good braking technique before you try to solve your troubles by throwing high-tech equipment at them. Use both front and rear brakes, applying them evenly and smoothly. Put more pressure on the front brake if you are going downhill and you are on smooth, clean, dry pavement. If the surface is slippery, use the brakes evenly and with great caution; don't ever let the bike pick up too much momentum. Do that gentle whisk-off before you brake in wet conditions, too. It improves the braking power of even the best pads in the rain.

Racks, Packs, and Carriers

You can use your ten-speed on more errands if you can carry things like groceries; if you can carry lunch and tools or a brief-case, you can ride to work. The following list of load-carrying gadgets runs from the simplest and cheapest to the strongest and most expensive. If you need to carry great big loads, or heavy loads *and* small children, consider the alternative bikes in Chapters 9 and 10.

But to carry just a book and a binder, or a sack lunch, or a carton of eggs and a few sundries, use a little cloth backpack like the one shown in Illustration 4. It has only one problem; you can't put much in it. Also, if you put something like a sack of peaches in there and then lean forward to shift your gears or get down low for reduced wind resistance, all of the peaches will roll forward out of the bag, bounce off the back of your

Illustration **4**

Cloth Backpack

noggin, and fall to the ground, leaving a colorful trail of splotches along the roadside. You can use a big safety pin (a diaper pin works great) to close the top of the pack, but this makes its capacity even more limited.

A good rack will carry much more than the little backpack, especially if you learn a few tricks about attaching things to it. The two most common types of rack that attach to the back end of the bike are shown in Illustration 5.

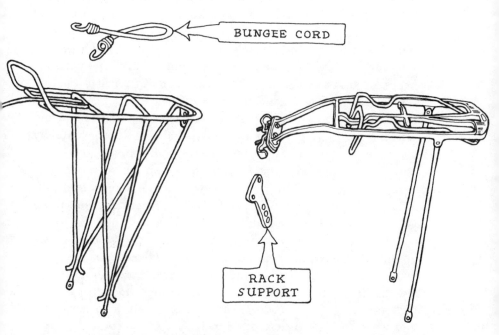

Illustration **5**   Brake Bolt-mounted and Standard-type Racks

The inexpensive type, exemplified by the Pletscher carrier, is heavier than the other type, and it has the nasty habit of working loose at the point where it is attached to the seat stays. Once it gets loose, it often slides down and squeezes your back brake on so the bike is a pain to ride. This problem can be taken care of by using a support such as the one shown. Put the rack clamp bolts through the two top holes in the T-shaped support. Then loosen the nut on the brake-mounting bolt, put this bolt through one of the bottom holes in the T, and tighten everything up really well (making sure your brake is still aligned so that the rim runs in the center of the space between the brake pads). The rack will now be much steadier, and even if it comes loose, it *can't* fall down on the brakes. You can get the rack and its nifty support from most bike shops or from any of the good catalogues (see Addresses). If you want to make sure the bolts and nuts stay tight, put a thread adhesive like Loctite on each bolt before screwing the nut on.

There are several rear racks that get a little more strength and stability by attaching directly to the brake-mounting bolt. They look more or less like the second model shown in Illustration 5, and they'll hold up anything from your briefcase to a fully loaded pair of pannier bags. They cost about twice as much as the old standard rack, but they are more reliable in the long run, especially if you use thread adhesive such as Loctite to keep the bolts and nuts tight. When you get a heavy load on them, though, it will tend to wag the back of the bike around, like a tail wagging the dog. This is annoying, and will bend and weaken the joint of the rack and the bike until it eventually breaks. If you want a super-solid rack for all types of loads, you have to get one like the Blackburn stay-mounted model discussed on page 57. This rack is costly and sometimes tricky to attach to your bike, but if you want to get serious about using your bike for all your errands and work, it's the only way to go.

To hold things onto your rack, whatever type you use, you'll need a couple of elastic bungee cords like the one in Illustration 5. If you keep a couple of bungee cords of different lengths (like a ten-incher and a sixteen-incher) hooked onto the rack frame, you can use one or both to strap down anything you want to carry. Briefcases, lunch pails, and things like textbooks are a breeze, especially if the bungee cords are used to hold down both ends of the load. Other bulgy or fragile loads may require putting a little flat piece of plywood (so things don't sag through the rack frame and rub the wheel) or even a box on the rack. If you come across a box that's a convenient size, keep it right near where you store your bike, so you can grab it and strap it on whenever you go shopping. A guy I know named Don Hall uses this handy wicker basket; his method is described on page 61 if you want to try it.

If you have to carry lots of dense, heavy stuff like piles of books or bottles of liquid or sacks of fruit and produce, the tail-wagging-the-dog problem will get to you. There are three other options you can try. You can get a pack that fits under your seat, and/or get another pack that fits between your handlebars, or you can convert your ten-speed to an upright-riding bike and put a big wire basket on the front, as described in Chapter 6. It's a lot more work to convert the bike to a sit-up model, but you'll wind up with much less of a tail-wagging problem, and you'll be able to carry weight on either or both ends of the bike without any difficulty balancing it. Sad to say, your own non-wagging tail may get sore if you ride farther than ten miles at a time in that upright position.

If you decide to keep your drop-bar ten-speed riding position and get either a handlebar or a seat pack, shop around and get good ones. They'll cost anywhere from two to ten times as much as the old standard bike rack, but they'll do a great job if they are designed and made well.

The good seat packs have a capacity of over 250 cubic inches, and they're made so you can get things in and out of them easily. They should also hang from the loops at the back of the seat in such a way that they don't swing forward and bump against the backs of your thighs as you pedal along. Those gentle nudges from behind might sound alluring at first, but on a ride of any distance at all, they bug you to distraction. To make sure your seat pack stays still and out of the way, you may have to make a couple of alterations in its mounting apparatus.

First, does your seat have those loops for the top straps of the pack? Many racing and some touring seats don't have those loops. You can add them by putting a sew-up clamp on the rails and cutting the rubber strap off so the pack straps can go through the loops. This will work for light packs only. For a stronger rack hanger, you can buy clamp-on loops from Bikecology (see Addresses) or make your own hanger, like the one Mark Newcomer designed for *Bicycling* magazine.

It consists of only a little flat bar of aluminum, measuring about 5½ by ¾ by ⅛-inches. You can buy flat bar stock in those dimensions from a big hardware or industrial supply store. While you're there, get a couple of really small U-bolts, the type they use to clamp ⅛-inch steel cables together. Round off the ends of the bar with a file, then drill rows of holes and file them into the loops for the pack straps to go through. To attach the bar to your seat rails, carefully mark and drill holes so the U-bolts can

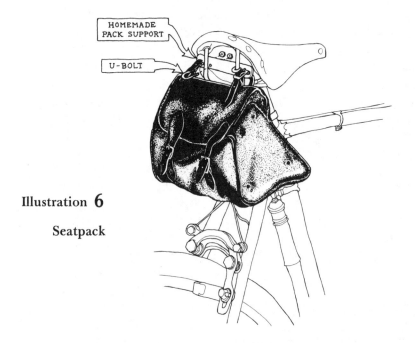

HOMEMADE PACK SUPPORT

U-BOLT

Illustration 6

Seatpack

go around the rails and through the bar as shown. Then take the U-bolt clamps apart and throw away the funny-shaped little piece with the notch in it for squeezing the cable. Push the ends of the U-bolts around the rails and through the bar (you can pinch or widen the U ends if they don't quite fit) and tighten the nuts on thoroughly. The whole thing is so simple and looks so professional, it's a wonder nobody has gotten the idea around before.

Once you've got strong loops to hang the pack from, the next thing you have to alter is the bottom of the pack, to keep it from swinging back and forth. The simplest solution is to sew two loops (one loop will do if you're lazy) onto the bottom of the bag; run a really short (6-inch) bungee cord from a loop down to the brake bridge, under the bridge, and back up to the other loop on the bottom of the bag.

The better handlebar packs, like the one shown in Illustration 7, will have a capacity of at least 400 cubic inches, a light and simple stem support that slides in and out of the pack, a stiff inner web construction that won't sag down and let the pack rub on the front wheel, and two bungee cords that stretch down to the drop-out eyelets on the front fork. If you don't have those eyelets on your bike, hook the bungee cords on the ends of the axle or around the lever and the little wire loop of your quick-release. If you have a QR without the little wire loop, take a strong pair of pliers and squish the wire hook at the end of the bungee cord into a long, skinny U-shape as shown in Illustration 8, then slip it around the flat dropout plate below

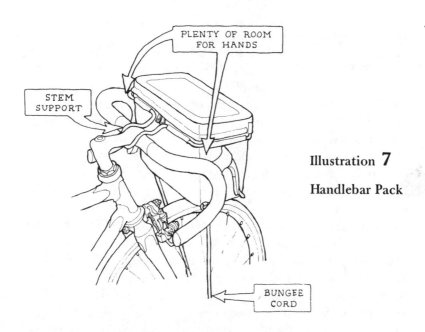

PLENTY OF ROOM
FOR HANDS

STEM
SUPPORT

BUNGEE
CORD

Illustration **7**

Handlebar Pack

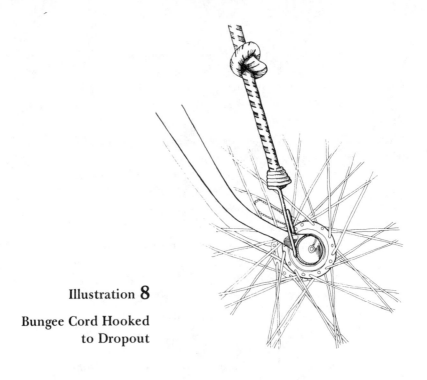

Illustration **8**

Bungee Cord Hooked
to Dropout

the rounded end of the fork blade. If the cords are loose because your bike is smaller than the standard size, just tie a knot in each of the bungee cords to tighten them up.

Make sure your handlebar pack is narrow enough so it won't touch your hands when you're riding; some handlebars are much narrower than others, and you may even have to change to wider bars to avoid the nagging feeling that your hands are being closed in and jostled as you ride along.

If you get a nice handlebar pack for short errands around town, but don't want it anywhere near your hands on a long ride, you can get a little gizmo called a "Seat Post Thing" from catalogues (see Addresses) or touring specialty shops. The SPT clamps onto your seat post and makes a T behind it, where the handlebar pack may be hung backward, out of the way. Alas, the pack will tend to wag your tail if you put heavy things in it back there. Tail-wagging or hand-cramping—you pays your money, and you makes your choice. For my money, I chose a little backpack and a super-sturdy rack like the Blackburn one in Chapter 6.

Wheels

When you're doing short errands and commuting around town, you do a lot of accelerating and braking. If the wheels on your bike are heavy steel ones, it takes extra work to speed them up and slow them down. Wheels with heavy steel rims are like big flywheels; they should be avoided, just like those big heavy tires discussed in the Tire section above. They have too much inertia. Your bike will feel a lot more spunky and sporty if you change the rims as well as the tires, to get as light a combination as is feasible. But changing the rims is much more expensive than pulling off the old rubber and putting on snazzy new light and narrow tires. It's best to have a real ace wheel-builder put new rims on your wheels. If you want to do the job yourself, get a good book like Robert Wright's *Building Bicycle Wheels,* and follow the instructions exactly, so you don't wind up with wheels shaped like eggs or potato chips.

Choose aluminum rims that are light and narrow (20–22 mm), but make sure you get ones with a reputation for strength. The standard-setting rims in this category are made by Super Champion; the Gentleman 20 mm and the two-tube construction 22.2 mm are both excellent. Use *strong* spokes, too; heavy straight 14-gauge, high-carbon, zinc-plated steel ones like those made by Union are great and fairly cheap. Or you can spend a little more and get butted 14-15-14-gauge, high-grade chrome/nickel stainless spokes such as those made by DT of Switzerland. The extra you pay for that fine Swiss steel is worthwhile; it takes only one broken spoke to foul you up if you're in a hurry to get someplace, or out riding a long way from the nearest bike shop.

Cranks and Other Components

You can lower the weight of your bike by replacing such steel parts as cranks, pedals, handlebars, stem, and seatpost with lightweight aluminum components. If you have cottered steel cranks and you have trouble with them coming loose and going ka-chunk, ka-chunk every time the pedals go around, save up some money and get a good set of cotterless aluminum cranks and chainwheels. Save another bunch, and you can get a great sealed bottom bracket set like the Phil Wood one; with the sealed bearings and the good cotterless cranks, you'll never have trouble with the front end of your power train again. No kidding. I have put my set through every sort of torture conceivable, and it has not made the slightest squeak, ker-chunk, or grumble. That, to me, is the definition of heaven on earth. And you don't have to pay a huge price for your cranks. There are perfectly useable cranks that cost less than half the price of the hand-polished fancy ones.

Don't spend piles of money on other super-light components, either. Unless you are a world-class time trial rider, you don't need to spend all that money to save just a few ounces. I mean, a hundred and fifty bucks for a titanium chain that saves you about an ounce-and-a-half of weight—that's CRAZY! You can make a much more significant weight-saving effort by visiting the rest-room before you hop on your bike, and think of the money saving you do while you're in there!

Frame

The frame is the bike's heart and soul. And it is its most expensive part, as I've written before. If you have a ten-speed with a frame that is much heavier than the frames of all the other bikes around, think about getting a whole new bike, or a used bike with a lighter, more lively frame. Weight does *not* equal strength in the world of bicycle frames. Some of the strongest bikes are made with high-grade steel butted tube frames, or thin straight-gauge tube frames. They are very light; the frames often weigh less than five pounds, but they can put up with enormous stresses. These strong, light frames cost four, five, or six times as much as the heavy clunker frames on discount-store bikes. They are, after all, the product of lots of fine craftsmanship, steel, and heat. Those things all carry inflated prices these days, but if you buy a great bike frame, at least you can think of it as a long-term investment. If you get a bike that fits you and does everything you need, you can keep it for your entire life. How many other costly things last that long? And how many costly things will be as useful to you?

So tighten your belt, set your jaw, and save up a big pile of money before you look for a new or used first-class bike frame. And before you run out and blow your big pile of money on some shiny, racy-looking thing with pretty holes drilled in all its secret parts, learn a bit about how frames are made and what the different designs are best suited for. Read the chapter on frames, written by master builder Al Eisentraut, in *Bike Tripping* (Ten Speed Press), or read through the little book *Bicycle Frames* by Joe Kossack (World Publications). Don't buy a super-stiff frame with steep angles and an almost rakeless straight fork, unless you intend to do criterium racing on smooth-swept streets and not much else. If you live in an area with some bumpy streets or if you intend to do some long rides out in the country, get one of the longer touring-style frames. They usually have eyelets for things like pumps, water bottles, and pack racks, and they often have a very responsive feel to them, even if they don't look quite as racy as the criterium-type bikes.

Gears

If your bike feels sluggish and you have made sure it doesn't feel that way because of soft tires, dry chain, loose rack, or heavy components, you may think that your bike is sluggish because it doesn't have the right gears. Think again. Unless it is a real specialized racing machine, it will have a range of gears that is fine for all normal riding situations.

It's wrong to think that you can go up mountains faster with Alpine gears. Extra-low gears make the bike go *slower* at any given rate of pedaling. Some Alpine gears (twiddlers, we call them) are so low that even when you pedal at a good brisk pace, you can't make enough headway to keep your balance. All your wobbling back and forth to balance slows your progress up the hill, and wears you out faster. As if that isn't enough of an indictment against twiddler gears, they also make the chain too loose, so the whole gear system gets erratic and quirky.

Don't worry about gears. Ride more, worry less about gears, and you'll soon find yourself torching up the hills. It's a simple matter of perseverance. If you want freedom from dependence on OPEC, you have to earn it. That doesn't mean you have to rush out and lunge fanatically at every hill in sight, like those manic mountain-men of the race circuit. It means something much harder. It means you must accept the fact that you're going to be quite slow on the hills at first. You may even be a bit ploddy when you're in your best condition. But you can do it, all yourself, and if you learn the joy and the pride of that sort of self-fulfillment, you'll be able to laugh at OPEC, twiddler gears, and lots of other hogwash.

Consider the Chinese cyclists. There are about 700 million of them, and almost all of them use bikes with one gear. Those bikes weigh over 50 pounds, unloaded. When they come to a hill, the Chinese get off and walk up it. My 40-pound three-speed seems like a luxury compared to that. Any ten-speed is sheer bliss by comparison. I have gotten into the habit of taking certain hills at a very slow, easy pace, so I can look at things that are growing along the roadside, or turn to look back at the view the higher elevation affords me. I don't need Alpine gears to get high on hills, any more than I need drugs. Getting to the top of a hill is a high all its own. Especially when you do it all on *your* own.

Illustration 9

Low Gears; American and Chinese

This may seem to be a slow and primitive sort of enjoyment to you, trudging or grinding the pedals upward. Pushing a bit on the accelerator of a car seems much more advanced. But the times they are a-changing. Pushing or pedaling a bike to the top of a hill appeals to me much more than stewing, griping, arguing, or maybe even pushing a car to the front of a long gas line. Especially when you have to watch all the other gasaholics in line as they bitch and fight and gripe among themselves in an effort to speed their progress in the line. What is slower? What is more primitive? What could possibly be more humiliating?

Enough digression. Leave your gears alone as long as they work OK. Ride up the hills that are rideable in your lowest gear, and walk up those rare ones that are too steep. As you get stronger, you'll get prouder and prouder about the steep hills you conquer. In a year of steady riding, you'll progress from walking up many hills to riding up almost all of them, and even starting to use your second or third gear on hills you used to think were impossible. Mountains won't become molehills, but they'll take on human, attainable proportions when you build up the strength and patience that come with experience. That combination of strength and patience is your greatest resource; it means you can not only beat the hills, but handle lots of other things in this frustrating, shortage-plagued world.

Chapter 3
Getting Around Safely

LET'S SAY your bike works fine, and you can ride it well, even if you have to walk up a steep hill now and then. The only thing that keeps you from enjoying your independence from gas and the automobile is your TERROR of those roaring, lurching, swerving, smogging gas-gulpers that rule the road.

If you need some help with the basic rules of the road for bicycles, read the Safety and the Safe Bike chapter in *Bike Tripping* (Ten Speed Press) or contact a local law enforcement agency and read the booklets they have on bike safety. There are a few basic regulations you should know cold before you venture out into traffic.

But if you want to use cycling as your main way of getting around, you can't just adjust your brakes so they're up to snuff, ride on the right side of the road, stop at stop signs, and expect to feel completely safe. In fact, when you start riding a lot in traffic, for a while it seems like every new situation you come into is more threatening than the last. Those car drivers seem to be out to GET you.

You have to go at cycling differently than they go at driving their cars. To be free of your fear of those unpredictable four-wheeled behemoths, stay away from them when possible. When you have to travel in close proximity with cars, make eye contact with their drivers, so they will be more predictable.

It's easy to say you'll try to stay away from cars; doing it is much harder. The more cars there are, the harder it gets. You have to learn all kinds of little tricks. Learn to pull over when you hear or see a wide truck or RV looming up behind you on a narrow road. Learn the traffic patterns in your area, and route yourself around the traffic jams that build up at the peak rush hours. Learn when the most dangerous drivers are on the roads; in most places this means Friday evening and Saturday afternoon and evening, when people tend to drink too much and drive like idiots. Learn special routes that are practical for bikes only, such as routes across empty parking lots, through parks, along river levees, and over unusual terrain that is closed to cars. This last business can become a real adventure. When you get a few basic commuting and shopping routes worked out, keep exploring alternatives for different situations.

For instance, if a certain street is crowded because all the workers in a plant are getting off the job, see if you can cut down a side street, take a parallel back street, and go through a park to return to your route toward home. If you have to get across a river and the main bridge has six lanes of traffic on it, traveling at fifty miles per hour even though the speed limit is thirty-five, maybe you can find a nearby pedestrian bridge, and ride over it slowly so as not to upset the pedestrians.

If there is a bottleneck on a particularly busy city street, you can often find an alley nearby. Use it carefully, avoiding any glass or sharp debris you come across. In some situations, it may even make more sense to get off the jammed street and ride slowly along the sidewalk, watching out for people walking around blind corners or stepping out of doors. In some busy intersections, the only way you can get through safely is to get off the bike and walk in the crosswalks with the other pedestrians.

Just make sure you don't break the law in using any of the various options open to you. I mean, it isn't so bad to noodle slowly along a deserted sidewalk, even if it is technically forbidden, as long as you don't get in the way of pedestrians. But it is horrible, unforgivable, and moreover bad for the cyclist's image, if you do things like making illegal left-hand turns. Only a foolish cyclist weaves through traffic to the wrong side of the street before getting to an intersection, then darts around the corner into oncoming cars. That idiot deserves any ticket or crack-up he or she gets.

The challenge on a bike is not seeing how far you can bend or break the law, but seeing how much you can do within the realm of safe cycling to keep up a steady pace toward your goal. It *can* be done, and when you learn to do it well, you'll often move as fast as the cars and buses that get all tied up in traffic snarls. The feeling of going faster than they, under your own steam, is a real ego-booster. If you get in good shape and are riding a light bike, you may even go fast enough to get right out in the street and take a lane in some situations, like on a one-way street. In most cities it is legal for a bike to take a lane where there is no room at the roadside, as long as you don't hold up traffic. Car drivers may resent seeing you out there in a lane (mostly out of jealousy), but at least they do see you.

I can and do take a lane for safety now and then, but that approach doesn't appeal to me nearly so much as finding some neato route around the traffic. The shortest way home may not be a straight line. And the circuitous route will often be more interesting, and much safer to boot.

But no matter how well you plan your route, there will be times when you can't avoid the traffic. And at those times, keep your eye on it, at every single second. This requires a lot of swiveling your head around. You may want to try using a mirror to make the job easier. There are little ones that clip or wire onto your glasses, your cycling cap, or your helmet; the ones made by Michael Benthin (see Addresses) are especially fine, but there are other good models available at bike shops and through catalogues that specialize in bike touring. Some catalogues also carry mirrors that can be attached to your handlebars. If you get a round three-inch handlebar mirror and then go to a car parts store, you can buy a wide-view convex mirror and stick it onto your bike one; this wide-view mirror will work even when you turn the handlebars, and it will not be so blurry when the bike is vibrating on rough surfaces.

But the danger for the cyclist is not so much that a car will come up from behind and swack him; the greater danger is that a car coming toward him or passing him will turn across his path without ever seeing him. The best defense is to watch not only the cars but also the drivers, so you can tell if they see you before your paths cross.

There are three especially dangerous situations where this method must be used. The first is a car passing a cyclist just before an intersection, then turning right, cutting off the biker. It seems unbelievable that the car driver doesn't see the cyclist while passing, but it happens all the time. So be ready for it. As you come to an intersection, slow down and watch the cars passing you, with your hands on the brakes so you can stop in a hurry if a car starts to cut you off. If you are a fast rider, approach the intersection with more speed and merge into the through traffic lane, so you can flow through the intersection with the other cars that aren't turning. Neither method is foolproof, especially when traffic is heavy and drivers are in nasty moods, but if you act firmly, decisively, and yet politely, you can always get through the critical moment of decision without getting run over or bugging the motorists unduly. The worst approach is to ride along slowly in the right turn lane, weaving indecisively, then take off from the curb at the last second to wobble out into the intersection. Car drivers hate that sort of act, and I don't blame them. If you merge through that turn lane with clear, firm resolve, they may not like you, but at least they'll know that you are going to get out of their way quickly.

Parked cars and cars coming out of blind driveways are another grave danger. There is only one solution. Keep a sharp eye out, and keep your speed down so you can stop quickly if necessary. What do you watch for? When riding right next to a row of parallel-parked cars, look for the heads of people who may be about to swing the door open and get out. When riding behind a row of diagonal-parked cars, watch for those white back-up lights; they mean the car is in reverse and ready to back up. As you approach a blind driveway, look for the front left fender of a car or truck. That's the fender that will get you, so it's the one you want to see coming. If you can see the whole car coming out of a driveway, look to see if the driver has spotted you, or is just craning his neck, gazing up and down the street without recognizing your existence at all. The split second you see one of these oblivious drivers coming out of a driveway, go for the brakes and start figuring out where you can go if the idiot keeps right on coming out into the street. Even if you can't stop, you may be able to slow down enough to turn and zoom into the driveway along the side of the car.

Buses tend to pull in and out of their stops at the curb without much regard for cyclists, too. When you see that there's a bus stop ahead, as you cross an intersection glance back and see if a bus is coming. If one is, merge out to the edge of the traffic lane so you won't get squished to the curb. If there aren't any cars in that traffic lane, go all the way into it so the bus can pull in beside you. If you are polite like that, you'll find that the drivers always see you and are good at avoiding you. They only treat you like dirt when you ignore them and dawdle around in their way. If, for instance, you come to a bus stop where a bus is loading, and you can see that the last passengers have gotten aboard, either hurry up and pass the bus or hang back and let the driver have a clear shot at pulling away from the curb. If you ride along the same bus route every day, and show politeness and decency to the poor beleaguered bus drivers, they'll get to know you and they'll be much less aggressive to you.

The third major danger of poor visibility for the cyclist is during dusk and darkness. If you don't have lights and reflectors at night, you are going to get hit. It isn't even a question of whether you'll get hit, it's a question of how soon. I avoid riding at night if I can, but when I had a job that didn't get off until after sundown, I used two of those nice little leg-band lights and made sure I had good, clean reflectors. Most new

WONDER LIGHT

LEG LIGHTS

Illustration **10**   Night Riding Lights

bikes now carry lots of reflectors, but the leg lights are still the best protection because they are bright even if the car's headlights miss them, and they bob up and down, which makes them extra-obvious. For still more visibility at the front of the bike, use a little "Wonder" light like the one shown. But even with all the bike-size lights and reflectors in the world, you may be invisible to some drivers; they're looking for big headlights, and they often ignore little blurs and glitters. If you want to go to an extreme, you can get a Belt Beacon, which is a big orange flashing thing that NO motorist can miss. It may drive you crazy it's so bright and strobe-like, but at least you'll know it makes you visible to those car drivers, even if you're driving down Main Street with a background of flashing neon signs!

So, you know how to make yourself visible to cars, and how to watch for them in tricky situations. But what do you do when the driver can see you perfectly, but still bears down on you like you are a target in a gunnery range? There are relatively few motorists who take pleasure in scaring cyclists off the road, and there are even fewer who hop into their cars when they are in really malicious, drunken, destructive states of mind, but it takes only one terrible driver to cause a fatal crash for a cyclist. The question is, how can you spot a bad or dangerous driver before he or she has taken a bead on you and run you down?

YOU LOOK 'EM IN THE EYE, PARDNER

When you confront a car in an intersection, and you know that your paths will cross, look hard at the driver's eyes, see if he or she looks back, and then make some sort of signal, a nod for the car to go ahead, or a smile and a little toss of your head in thanks if the driver indicates that you can go ahead.

This may sound weird and silly to a seasoned car or truck driver who is just starting to use a bike. When you're in a car, you poke the nose of the thing out, and when you see another car slowing down, you floor the gas pedal and shoot out into the traffic. Why all this batting of eyes back and forth, and little jerks of the head and smiles?

It's a matter of survival. When you're riding a bike, you can't count on a big metal proboscis to stick out into the traffic and tell other people where you want to go and when. On a bike, you can't isolate yourself from other drivers; you can't push down an accelerator to shoot past them, either. There has to be more give and take. If you can see by looking at a driver's eyes that he or she is the type to SNATCH the right of way, the type that sticks the snout of the car out there and refuses to make eye contact with any measly cyclist, then you give way, and let the so-and-so go, and attempt to make better eye contact with the next driver. When you see a clearly polite reaction from a driver you can ride ahead, confident that you will be given clear passage. You'll learn to size up drivers quickly, then make a sure, safe decision about whether to go in front of them or let them take all the road they want.

An obvious corollary to the eye contact theory is that if a car is going so fast that you can't even get a glimpse of the driver's eyes, then stay out of the car's path. This means, in turn, that you can't be going too fast to stop in any situation where you may come across one of those hell-bent drivers. You can't go through intersections with main thoroughfares at more than about fifteen miles an hour. Even at that speed, you should look ahead for any possible trouble that might develop as you go into the intersection, trouble like a car turning right or left to cut across your path, or a pedestrian who might step into the street and make things complicated.

In some cases, where there is heavy, complex traffic, and you can tell right off that no car drivers are going to take the time to make eye contact, the only ways to get through are to get in the "shadow" of a car and let it run interference for you, or, if you aren't speedy and confident enough for that method, just go to the curb, get off the bike, and walk through the intersection, using the crosswalks and WALK signals. This can be especially helpful in a big intersection if you want to make a left-hand turn; you can ride through the intersection on the street you've been following, then stop at the corner, get off, push the button and take off to your left when the light changes.

But this slow method is necessary only in the most drastic situations. If you have a light bike and are in good shape, you will often be able to pick your way through intersections even faster than the cars. This can get funny if you are riding across town; you keep passing and being passed by the same cars. You hold a steady, relaxing pace of fifteen to twnety miles per hour, and they lunge up to forty, then have to slam on their brakes when the traffic backs up at the next red light.

All that lunging and squealing doesn't get them to the other side of town any quicker, and the toll it takes on car, tires, gas, engine, air quality, and nerves is all out of proportion.

Keep this in mind if you ever feel that you aren't going fast enough on your bike. You can't get the same power rush on a bicycle that you can from an accelerating gas-gulper, but you do get a different sort of thrill every time you pass a mess of gas-hogs all clogged up in a traffic jam. It's more than the fact that you have figured out a nicer, quicker way to get around town. It's that you have kicked the high-power travel habit. You are no longer a gasoholic.

The meaning of this freedom from gas addiction will grow on you. You will start to feel better each time you ride across town, even if you don't get there faster than a car. The trip may take you five minutes longer, but then you may live five or ten years more of a happy, healthy life if you keep cycling regularly. Isn't that a good trade-off?

And take a look at the condition of the gasoholics! As you do your eye contact with them, notice that strange look in their eyes; it's a distant, bland stare. They look hooked, spaced out, stoned on the whole big-car, go-fast trip. You have to watch out for them when they look that way; they may be oblivious to your presence and right-of-way. Or they may actually be stoned on something more directly mind-bending than driving an auto-mobile.

Now, most motorists would object to being compared with common drug addicts and alkies. But when you're riding a bike, you can see one effect of gasoline addiction that is quite similar to the effects of booze and drugs. They all make the user stare like a senile octogenarian. They all limit the quality of sensory input. A strung-out driver will watch the road dead ahead, and perhaps look to the side if a large, glittering object like a 1959 Lincoln Continental looms up from a side street, but he or she will not bother to focus on lesser objects that blur past, like small shrubs, miniature poodles, or cyclists.

So you have to watch out for them. Give those spaced-out petrol junkies plenty of room. This may mean dodging off the pavement, or stopping very quickly at an intersection, or darting up a nearby driveway.

All these escape tactics sound scary. You don't have to be paranoid, though. If you are wide awake and using all of your senses when you ride, you can spot or hear or smell (bus exhaust does give you a distinct olfactory warning) the traffic problems before they are a threat. To me, part of the fun of riding around town is using all my senses, not only to detect approaching dangers, but also to pick up little sensory delights that motorists miss. I go by Mrs. Gunther's garden in spring, and a wave of fragrance from her freesias engulfs me. I pedal past Mr. Eddy's at about six in the evening, and hear him yelling to his wife as she fries up some sausage for dinner. I pass the school and watch the kids playing in the yard, then hear that happy, furious racket they make for the next block or so.

In a way, the use of your senses can be even more refreshing than the physical exercise you get while doing errands on your bike. If you get up from work and cycle downtown to get some paper or a book or a tool or something, you return to your job refreshed and more alive. If you take a car, you come back dazed, frustrated by the traffic and parking hassles, and in no mood to work at all.

Don't get smug about your superior and more enjoyable mode of transit, though. If you ride too close to the cars, using their routes so you can lord over them, racing them and demanding your equal lane space, the main sensory treats you'll discover are the stink of smog and the rasping cough that is brought on by inhaling too much exhaust. What's worse, you may rediscover your weight disadvantage in some sudden and awful way, like, for instance, when a car runs you down.

There are serious cyclists around these days who suit up with motorcycle helmets and gas masks for riding through heavy traffic. It makes sense if you have to commute through the heart of a city twice every day. But to me, it goes against the whole sensory advantage you get on a bike. You can get gas masks and heavy-duty helmets from some of the catalogues (see Addresses), but it makes more sense for your senses to find less smoggy and trafficky routes so you can enjoy them without fear or injury or inhalation. All you need for this sort of route is a light one like the Hair Net type on page 32.

If you commute to work and have to get there early in the morning, you may pick a route that is utilitarian and fairly direct, even one that includes busy streets. Most drivers are pretty sane on their way to work, and the air is more clear at that hour. If there are one-way streets with no-parking zones along the curb, you can ride there, at a good clip, without having to worry about the door of a parked car opening in your face.

On your way home from work, when you aren't in a rush and you need to unwind a little, try a less direct, prettier route, like a bike path that winds through a park or along a beach or river.

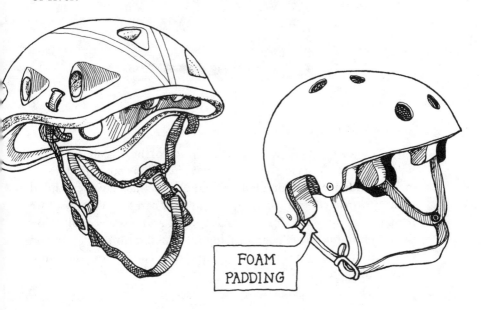

FOAM
PADDING

Illustration **11**   Hard Shell and Motorcycle Type Helmets

No matter how good your routes and riding techniques, do wear some sort of helmet if you ride around in traffic a lot. All of the nasty statistics compiled by state and federal agencies agree that the worst injuries to cyclists are often head and neck injuries. Bad trauma to the head is even more common among ten-speed cycling victims than it is among riders on sit-down bikes. This is logical, since on a ten-speed your head is jutting out like a battering ram in front of the bike. For a safer cycling position, take a look at the recumbent bike on page 143. But if you're going to stick to your standard ten-speed, get a good helmet.

Hair Net Helmet

You can get all types and qualities of headgear, from the light "hair net" style that racers have used for so long, to specially-molded and padded hard-shell helmets that have descended from motorcycling equipment. No helmet can give you absolute protection, but look for one that is light and has a combination of a high-impact shell, snug-fitting foam cell cushions, and good ventilation that doesn't whistle in your ears when the wind blows through.

Chapter 4
Solving the Problem of Flats

IT'S SO deflating. You're riding along, enjoying yourself, your bike, and your wide open surroundings, and then BWAM! Or maybe just SSSSSSSSSSSSSSSSsssssssssss, and you slow to a stop, then look down at the sad and hopeless shape of your tire. And you have to either take out your patch kit and tire irons to fix your perforated tube, or walk all the way home with the flat tire ka-thumping along forlornly.

As you change, fix, or ka-thump that tire to get home, you will wonder why all those cars passing you never get flats, but *you* seem to pick up a puncture about every third time you go for a bike ride. If you were on your way to work, you will be especially aggravated because the flat will make you late for the job.

You've got to get to the root of the problem and solve it. First figure out why you're getting so many punctures, then do a thorough job of putting together the right set of tubes, tires, and pumping gear for your needs. Learn some simple preventive riding techniques, too, so you can go riding without fear of getting a nasty flat.

If you have superthin racing sew-up tires, or very light and thin-treaded clincher (wire-on) tires, and you have to ride around a town where there are lots of little pieces of glass, metal, and other debris on the road, your problem is due to inadequately thick tires. See the Utility Tires section below.

If you have sturdy utilitarian tires, but still get flats from big nasty pieces of glass and metal, you may have to get Special Flat-proof Tires and Tubes as described in that section.

If your tires are always soft because you don't have a pump that can inflate them well, you're asking for flat trouble; soft tires spread out wider and are much easier to puncture. To keep your tires pumped up well, see the Pumps and Connectors section.

If you have good tires and tubes, but got a flat and repaired it and now have trouble with a leaky tube (maddening, isn't it?), your best bet is to start over with a new tube. Then get a good touring patch kit (the ones made by Flac and Rema are available at many shops and from the catalogues listed in Addresses). Learn how to patch your tires efficiently from a seasoned mechanic or a good repair manual such as *Anybody's Bike Book*.

When you've got your tires set up and inflated properly, you should also learn some Anti-debris Techniques so you can reduce your flats to one every couple of years or so; if you don't have any more than that, you'll be doing beautifully.

Utility Tires

There are bicycle tires for almost every purpose. There are super-light thin ones for racing on hardwood tracks, and there are solid noninflatable ones that can be ridden over glass all day without flats. But most riders need something in between those extremes. For most, the combination below will work like a charm. If your needs are for maximum lightness and perform-ance, you have to get the sew-ups. If you need superior dura-bility, see the Special Flat-proof Tubes section.

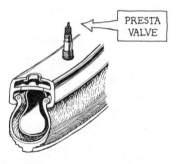

PRESTA VALVE

Illustration **12**

Profile of Utility Wheel

The utility tire, tube, and rim shown in Illustration 12 are chosen for a combination of lightness, strength, and practicality. The tire is narrow, a 27-by-1⅛-inch size that's about the same width as the rim. But there is a thick ridge of rubber tread along the center of the tire where it meets the ground. That's where you need the extra thickness when you run over a piece of glass; that's also where most wear is on the tire. Notice that the thin rubber coating covers the tire out to the widest point on the sidewall. This is good designing; it will prevent almost all cuts of the sidewall by sharp curbs and rocks scraping alongside. The tire bead or edge fits snugly inside the lip at the edge of the aluminum alloy rim, but the fit is not so tight that it's difficult to get the tire on and off the rim. Sad to say, some of the latest superlight utility tires are hard to get on and off some rims. Avoid these finger-busters unless you are a real expert at getting tires on and off rims without damaging the tube. The casing on the tire shown in Illustration 12 is double-reinforced nylon cord. This may make the tire a bit heavier than those superlight ones, but it means the tire can fit a little looser and it means the tire will produce a firm ride and great durability, even on gravel roads or bumpy pavement.

The tube is a high-pressure butyl type, with a Presta valve that's easy to use with a push-on air chuck on a frame pump or floor pump. You can use an adapter as described in the Pumps and Connectors section just below.

The rim and spokes shown are compatible with the tire. There is a narrow (20 mm) rim that is of a light but strong tubular-type construction. It should be laced to the hub with strong but light spokes, tightened up well so the whole wheel will absorb road shocks easily; it should not be so stiff that it delivers the shock up to you, but it should not be so loose that the tire and tube have to take the force of the blow. A good wheel will spread out the work, so the point of impact on the tire gets some help. Like, for instance, when you go over a pothole, the whole well-tensioned wheel should give and then spring back, so the whammy doesn't blammy the tire.

Pumps and Connectors

Your tires will be full of air only if you have a good pump and connector (or "chuck") to inflate them with. If you live near a good bike shop that caters to touring and racing cyclists, or if you get a good catalogue (see Addresses) and buy a solid floor-standing pump, keep it where you store your bike and you'll be sure to have well-inflated tires all the time. If you try to make do with a cheapo pump and one of these screw-on connectors that are made for car tires, you'll never be able to get the tires up to the proper pressure. And pumping up your tires makes such a difference; save up the necessary dough and get one of those spiffy long/thin cylinder pumps with an air gauge on it; with them, it's a breeze (heh) to blow the tires up to a good high pressure. Get a good frame pump, too. Many of the expensive ones have weak joints, so don't buy just by the price; seek out a frame pump that has a reputation for lasting.

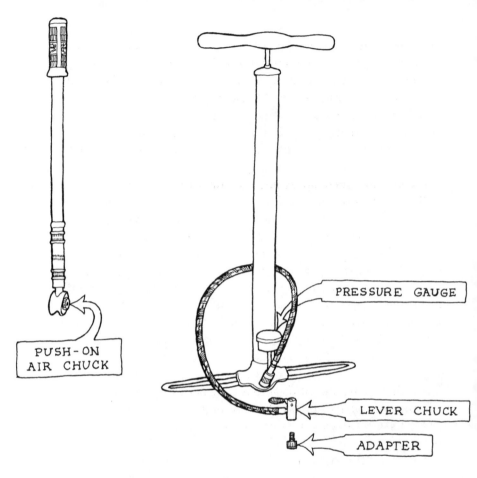

PUSH-ON
AIR CHUCK

PRESSURE GAUGE

LEVER CHUCK

ADAPTER

Illustration **13**   Presta-type Pumps

The floor and frame pumps will take care of almost all of your inflation requirements, but it's also good to carry an adapter such as the little screw-on type shown in Illustration 13. The ones with the long body like the illustrated model are for use with the types of pump chucks that either screw on or clamp on with a little hand lever. The adapter with the short sides is for use with the kind of gas station chuck that has a little peg on the end that must hit the valve point on your tire valve. Get the adapter that will be the most useful for the pumps around you.

The only trouble with these little things is that they are all too easy to lose. Take yours and hunt around your bike for a little bolt end that it can screw onto. The bolt of the clamp that holds your gear cable housings on the down tube is good, or maybe a bolt for your rear reflector or something. Screw the adapter on that bolt by hand (not too tight or you'll strip those soft brass threads) and you can forget all about it until that rainy day when your tire is flat and your frame pump is leaky or broken. Then you can smile and unscrew your little brass gem, use a gas station pump or a borrowed car tire pump, and get your tire filled up again; the sun will come out, the birds will start to sing, and you'll ride off thanking yourself for adding that little adapter to your bike's equipage.

If you have a bike with the standard Schrader valves like car tires have, switch the tubes to Presta and get a rubber grommet (like a little lifesaver with a slot around the perimeter) that will fit in the hole in your rim and make it smaller so the skinnier Presta valve will be snug in there. Why is it better to use Presta valves that you have to unscrew every time you pump up? Good question. The Presta valve will not leak after you screw it down tight. Schrader valves usually don't leak much, but it doesn't take much of a leak to make trouble for you on your bike. A whole lot of air has to leak out of a car tire before the pressure gets too low. On a bike, just a tiny leak will lower the pressure by ten or twenty pounds overnight. Losing that much air can slow you down by as much as twenty percent. So take a little time and trouble and get those Presta valves which don't leak.

The whole subject of tires and pumps and connectors can be summed up in one sentence; spend a little more time and money to get things set up right, and you'll save lots of trouble on the road.

Special Flat-Proof Tubes and Tires

These are alternatives to the utility set-up described above, for those of you who ride where junk on the roads is so bad that flats are driving you crazy.

All of the alternatives are heavier than the lighter models of pneumatic clincher tires, but the urethane tunnel tire is close to the weight of a medium-duty clincher-tube combination, so you don't have to pay for fewer flats with more weight in all cases. If you want to do a compromise to limit your flats, use a beefy flat-proof tube or tire on your rear wheel, and a lighter utility clincher on the front wheel so it can steer and respond to the road in that light, sensitive way that only a really light pneumatic tire can do. Most of your weight is on the rear tire, so that's where you have most of your flats. Flats are harder to change on the rear tire, too, so if you get rid of that possibility, you'll be saving yourself the bulk of your hassles.

The simplest remedy for minor puncture leaks is to put a thorn-proof tube in the tire you already have. The thorn-proof tube has a very thick wall of rubber on the outside. If you have a good utility tire with a ridge along the rolling surface, the combined thickness of tire and thorn-proof tube will prevent punctures in 99 cases out of 100. The tube weighs almost twice

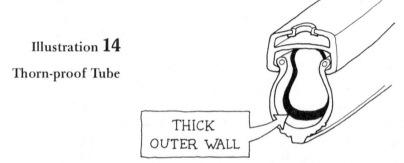

Illustration **14**

Thorn-proof Tube

THICK OUTER WALL

what the skinny lightweight ones do, and it's hard to mount. You have to inflate it a bit to shove it in there and get it lined up inside the tire with the thick side toward the ground. Then deflate it again so you can squeeze the second bead of the tire onto your rim without mangling that bulky tube. It's quite a tussle, but it's worth it if you don't get a flat for another year or so. In desert areas, where cactus thorns abound, it's the only way to fly.

Two slightly more drastic cures to the flat problem involve replacing your inner tube or your whole tire with a unit that does not hold air, but rather depends on a rubber ring for support and shock absorption. These alternatives are expensive, and they are harder to mount than any standard tire and tube combination, but they are completely puncture-proof, and that may be worth the money and effort if major puncture flats are a constant hassle for you.

Illustration **15**

Rubber Insert

INSERT

You can put a specially-formulated rubber insert in the tire you already have. This will add a pound-and-a-half or so to the weight of the wheel, and will cause a noticeable dampening of the bike's responsiveness if you use it on the front wheel. But if you can find exactly the right size of insert for your rim and tire, you can produce a useable substitute for an air-filled tube. To get the insert into your tire, remove one bead of the tire from the rim and take your old tube out, then cover the insert with a soap and water solution (mixed in a one-to-one ratio), and start stuffing the thing into the tire. Put both of the ends in first, holding them together with one hand while you use the other to push more of the insert into the tire and push the tire bead back onto the rim. This process is tricky even when the tire, rim, and insert are a perfect match. If you have a tire or rim that is narrower than the standard size (many of the new 27-by-1¼-inch rims are narrower these days) you may find it impossible to keep the bead of the tire around the insert and tucked into the rim. And all the soap and your sweat mixes together and makes it even easier for the tire bead to slip out on one side or the other, allowing that fat worm of an insert to wriggle free. It can turn into a Freudian nightmare if you don't keep your cool.

But if the insert is the right size, you'll be able to get it in with perseverance and maybe some help from a friend. The last few inches will be especially stubborn, but just take it slow and make sure you don't pinch the insert with any sharp tool that might cut it. A good idea is to push the last loop of the slippery thing into the tire *before* trying to get the last one-third of the bead onto the rim. Pushing the insert into place will compress it

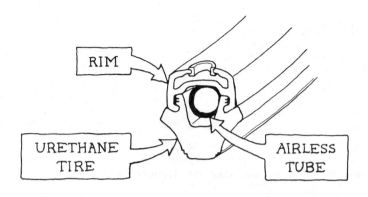

Illustration **16**   Tunnel Cushion Urethane Tire

all the way around the wheel, so you don't have to fight all that compression at the last section of tire. If the insert dries out as you work on it, slop more soapy water on, so it will slip easily against the inside of the tire; it has to be a very snug fit or the wheel will have a loose, sloppy feel.

Once the insert is installed, wipe the extra soapy water off the wheel and you can ride away, free of flats forever.

The last alternative to standard tires and tubes involves replacement of the whole unit with a urethane tire and a non-pneumatic inner tube. This combination is less expensive than the insert, but it requires a great deal of care in mounting. It's best to have someone with experience from a shop to help you mount the first one, so you'll know the tricks of how to do it without damaging the urethane and plastic parts. The good thing about the urethane "tunnel cushion" alternative is that it is *not* much heavier, and it even rides pretty much like a standard tire, due to the quality of the special urethane employed. It feels about like a very hard high-pressure clincher tire, except when you go over a pothole or large rock, or when you ride on bumpy pavement for a long time. The tunnel cushion can't take care of those extreme conditions. A pothole can deliver a jarring blow to the rim and bike frame, and riding on bumpy pavement can rattle your bones to bits over a long period. But unless you're a racer or long-distance rider, these limitations won't bother you much. If the road vibrations get to you, try wearing padded gloves, or using thick-padded handlebar tape, and a seat with two pads where your pelvic bones rest (see Illustration 26).

Anti-Debris Techniques

OK, let's say you've got good utility tires, and a good pump so you keep them inflated to the right pressure. Flats should never be a problem. But they are, if you have to ride through an area where there is lots of broken glass or debris along the shoulder of the road. I remember taking a long ride out to a big reservoir once, on a hot Saturday in May. All along that road, I was being passed up by these knuckleheads hauling their big gas-guzzling water-ski boats to the lake on trailers behind their big gas-guzzling hot-rod four-wheel-drive pickups. The lovely spring air was filled with the smog they poured out. What's worse, they were guzzling beer and filling the air, the roadside ditches, and my tires with their empties. By the time I had stopped to fix my second flat, my blood was at the boiling point, but when some howling yahoo leaned out of his car window and threw a bottle that smashed right at my feet, showering me with glass and left-over nitrosamines, I just about blew out my own tubes from a fit of hypertension.

To keep the pressure up in your tires and down in your cardiovascular system, avoid routes that are frequented by those gas-and suds-guzzling knucklehead types. But this avoidance can go only so far. You can watch for the little patches of glass at intersections, and ride around them carefully, and you can keep your eyes peeled for the telltale glint of glass or metal on the edge of the road ahead of you, but if there is more than a certain minimal amount of litter along the road, you're not going to be able to avoid all of it. You can get those little wire tack-pullers that skim along the tire surface, but they don't work on big sharp litter objects that slash the tire instead of getting stuck in it. You can get a nonpneumatic tire, but they all have limitations. There's no perfect substitute for an air-filled tire, so you may decide you have to use pneumatic tires, even in this litter-filled country.

The answer to the litter problem is simple to say, but much harder to achieve. You have to get together with other cyclists and people who hate litter, and get your state or federal representatives to pass a container recycling law, similar to what they have in Oregon. All beverage containers in Oregon are recyclable; you pay a deposit on each bottle or can, and get the deposit back when you return the container. Other cities and states

have similar laws, and the movement could turn into a national law if it could get enough momentum. Now, I haven't ridden a bike too much in Oregon, but when I did go cycling there, I couldn't believe how clean the roadsides were. And that went for city streets as well as highways out in the open country. It was like a dream come true. I didn't have to keep my eyes glued to the pavement twenty yards ahead of me, so I could keep a lookout on the traffic and get a better look at the great green Oregon scenery, too. What freedom! What a wonder of progress! What a contrast to California! All cyclists should push for can- and bottle-recycling laws, so they can enjoy clean roadsides like the ones in Oregon. It will take time and effort to overcome the throw-away ethic and the lobbying power of the container companies, but stick together and stick to it; a litterless future can be ours!

Chapter 5
Preventing Rip-offs

IT'S A bummer to talk about bike thefts. It reminds me of the time my beloved old Cinelli got ripped off. But if you have a ten-speed and you want to use it for all your commuting and shopping trips, you have to face the problem and work out a solution that's convenient enough so you'll always use it, and secure enough so you won't lose your bike unless a really exceptional desperado goes after it.

First, you have to figure out where the greatest threat of a rip-off is. If you ride to work in a big shop or an office in an area where theft is a way of life (this doesn't necessarily mean a poor neighborhood; if the area has lots of theft, though, you'll be sure to hear about it through friends and co-workers), you must find a place that is off the street, inside if possible, and provided with strong posts to lock your bike onto. If the working place has no secure bike storage area, get together with your co-workers who ride bikes, mopeds, and light motorcycles to work, and petition the management. Offer to work for free on the weekends to help put a roof over the storage area, or maybe even take up a collection to help defray the cost of bike storage. In the more civilized (that is, bike-conscious) countries of Europe, there is a bike storage room in every office and factory. In many parts of China, the people are so civilized they don't have to worry much about theft; they just use little frame-mounted locks. But here in America, you'll need a closed-in storage area. If you can't get that, the next best things are lockers. Some public office buildings put these up, if the folks in charge are enlightened. The lockers work well for bikes, but they take up lots of room, and they have a built-in risk; if they only cost a quarter to operate, local down-and-out gypsy folks begin to use them as storage bins or even houses! This is a sad state of affairs, and a pretty caustic comment on housing conditions, but it must be taken into consideration.

If you live in an area where there are many robberies, you have to be careful about where you put your bike at home. You may need to take it right into your house or apartment, and perhaps even lock it in your bedroom if it's a flashy new ten-speed with fancy components that would be easy to sell to a "fence" in the underworld. This is another ironic comment on the state of the human condition; you can't get bike lockers because bums keep making them into bedrooms, and you have to turn your own bedroom into a bike locker to keep thieves from stealing your bike!

If your life is replete with threats of thievery at both work and home, you may have to get two identical heavy locks and chains. You can leave one at home and one at work; then all you have to do is carry a single key with you when you commute, and you can feel secure without lugging your security devices around with you like so much extra baggage of paranoia.

If you ride your bike to a bus stop, especially a bus stop where you know lots of punky kids hang out while they're waiting for buses, you'll either have to find a locker for the bike, or lock the frame and wheels to a solid object, and be prepared to face severe vandal damage from time to time. There are many bus stops at which you simply can't leave a high-quality bike. You have to get a clunker to ride down to the bus stop, or find a safe place to lock your ten-speed that's a half-block or so away from the bus stop. If it's out of range of those punks who have nothing to do while they wait for the bus, they probably won't bother it.

If you make lots of quick errands on your bike, those few moments you take to dart into a store may be the time of greatest risk for your trusty two-wheeled companion. You must find some sort of lock and chain or cable arrangement that you can use to attach the bike's frame and wheels to either a post, a fence, a fire hydrant, or a bike rack. Try to pick a parking spot that's in a public, busy area; avoid dark corners and hidden nooks, especially if you see ominous clues of previous rip-offs, such as a wheel locked to a pole and the rest of the bike missing.

For all of the above locking situations, get the lock and chain or cable that will work best for your needs. For instance, if you are looking for locks and chains to leave at your house and at work, they don't have to be light and easy to carry; they can be big strong ones, like maybe a chain with $7/16$-inch-thick links, and a big solid padlock. Both chain and lock hasp should be of hardened steel, and, if possible, coated with vinyl so they won't scratch the paint on your bike frame.

If you want a locking system that you can carry around, you can get a chain or cable that's just big enough to go around your waist. Then you can lock it there, ride to your destination, take it off and lock both the wheels and frame of the bike to a solid post, and put the unit back around your waist to ride home.

You can either use a short chain, like the "biker" in the picture, or get a six-foot, $5/16$-inch cable that goes around your waist twice. The long cable can go through both wheels and the frame without requiring removal of the front wheel. You must make sure, though, that no part of the long cable can be pulled down near the ground; thieves using big clippers can use the ground for leverage and snip through your cable or chain in seconds unless it's up too high for the clippers to reach it while lying along the ground. The six-foot cable may not be long enough to reach around your body twice if you are big and hefty; either lose weight until the cable fits, or get a lock with a long hasp so the whole lock and cable unit will reach around you.

Hang your lock and waist-size chain or cable right next to where you store your bike at home, or use it to lock up your bike there, so every time you grab the bike to go on an errand, you won't forget to take the security system too.

There is another type of lock, known as the Kryptonite or Citadel, that clips onto the frame of the bike. It provides excellent security if you take off the front wheel and lock it to the rear wheel, the frame, and a post. But this type of lock is at least twice as expensive as any of the others mentioned above. If you have a really costly, shiny ten-speed and have to leave it for hours at a time in a high-risk area, you may find a high-cost lock worth the expense. In high-risk areas, though, leaving an eye-catching bike doesn't make sense anyway; the seat and handlebars may get stolen, or the tires slashed. I mean, if you're a punk and you see a really intimidating fancy bike, locked up with a really intimidating fancy lock, the whole scene makes you itch to wreak havoc. And if there's a will for havoc, there's always a way to wreak it.

In fact, no lock can protect a snazzy bike from the ire of a confirmed vandal, nor can it completely protect the bike from space-age thieves using stuff like super-low temperature freon, four-foot bolt cutters, and endless ingenuity. There is another approach you can take, though; make your bike less eye-catching.

When the wheels get a little dirty and dusty, leave them that way. If you get a few nicks and scrapes on the frame, paint them over with splotches of paint that don't quite match the original color. Take off most or all of your colorful decals. If you scratch off some paint in the process, don't worry; you can cover that with off-color touch-up paint, too. Get an electric hand engraving tool (police departments will often lend you one for free) and write your initials, state code letters, and driver's license number or social security number on the seat tube right under where it joins the top tube. If there's a decal right there

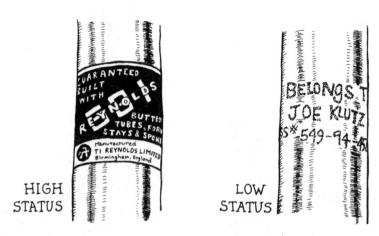

HIGH STATUS   LOW STATUS

Illustration **17**   Seat Tube Labels

that says what kind of fancy steel tubes the bike is made of, scratch off the decal and put the engraving there instead.

Boy, that lowers the status level of your bike. You may not want to degrade your bike that way. But why should *you* worry about that little tubing-decal symbol? *You* know your bike is made of good materials. You ride it; you know it feels good. You don't have to flaunt it.

Think of the bike as a tool instead of a status symbol. Do you worry about leaving the brand label on your hammer? Do you care if the trademark comes off your favorite pair of scissors? Of course not. As long as you keep those scissors sharp and rust-free, you'll be happy with them all your life.

The same logic can work for your bicycle. It doesn't have to look like a museum piece, as long as it is properly maintained and working well. Don't let it get rusty or broken-down, but don't worry about a bit of dust or splotchy touch-up paint; those dust and splotch-marks are like insurance when a thief is looking for something that will sell quickly to a fence, or when a punk is looking for something shiny to defile.

Illustration 18   Upright Walk-along Position

If you can't bear to de-glorify your beloved ten-speed, take it inside with you whenever possible. This can be awkward if you have to jockey through narrow doors, between cluttered desks, and into crowded elevators. To get around more gracefully, use an upright walk-along position, as shown on the previous page. Pull it up into that wheelbarrow position when you're still outside and have some room; just get the bike rolling as you walk next to it, then swing the handlebars up so the bike goes vertical and the rear wheel glides along in front of you. It may seem hard to balance at first, but soon you'll be able to whiz in and out of the house and office.

There is another alternative for local shopping and commuting trips. Get a funky clunker bike, a three-speed or even a one-speed, and use it when you have to leave a bike in the line of fire of punks and thieves. You can buy a clunker for thirty bucks or less at a garage sale, flea market, or used bike dealer, and you can use any old lock on it, leave it for hours at a time, and never have to worry a bit. See Part II of this book for more info on clunkers, three-speeds, and alternative bikes.

The only trouble with clunkers is that they ride clunky. Also, if you don't have lots of storage space at home, it's going to be hard to find a place for your second bike. To me, the slight added hassle of parking my second bike is more than worth the worry saved. My hot-shot ten-speed stays safe at home while I run errands on the three-speed. The only problem is that in some places clunkers have gotten to be status symbols in their own right (see page 121). If they get too precious, like Model A Fords or something, they may be harder to keep from thieves in the future.

Chapter 6
Fixing Up a Ten-Speed for Shopping

IT'S CRAZY to jump into a half-ton pickup to go pick up a half-pound of green beans at your local market. But there's also something crazy about riding to the market on your ten-speed and trying to carry home three full shopping bags on it. The scene gets really crazy when you try to reach down to your gear levers with both arms full of tomatoes, oranges, eggs, and other perishables. I mean, even the handlebars are much too far down there to be of any use to you. This chapter will cover two ways you can set up your ten-speed to be an efficient shopping vehicle. The first involves changing the basic riding position of the bike for convenience and stability. The second is a method for using the ten-speed as is, and adding carrying devices that will make it more of a workhorse bike. At the end of the chapter there will be a bunch of hints that can make the whole shopping-via-bike trip easier and more practical.

Converting to an Upright Riding Position

Let's put some cards on the table about the cycling position on a ten-speed. We all thought that racy low-slung look was great when we saw other people riding ten-speeds. But when we got on our own ten-speed bikes for the first time, we didn't feel so racy, did we? I remember finding that position much less comfortable than the way I sat on the trusty old clunker I had in my school days. And no matter how good a cyclist you were at the time, I bet you had a few wobbly moments the first time you tried to ride all bent over with your hands way down there on those low bars and your head sticking out front like a turtle's. Remember how hard it was to look around at traffic and weave your way through intersections, when you could hardly reach the brake and gear levers? And if you had to carry anything, it meant riding one-handed, and that was damn near IMPOSSIBLE.

My solution to the problem was to get a second bike, an old three-speed that reminded me of my school-days bike. It was easy to use around town, and easy to make into a real workhorse station wagon like the one on page 89. I have saved

49

the racy, lightweight ten-speed mainly for long joyrides out in the country. If you want to keep your ten-speed intact and get a shopping bike that's fairly inexpensive, but more sporty than an old clunker, you can buy a five- or ten-speed mixte-frame (unisex) bike. If you do the procedures in Chapter 9, you can come up with a sporty variation on the station wagon bike, as shown on page 83.

But if you have room to store only one bike where you live, and you never take the time to ride it out to the country, so it sits in the closet gathering dust while you use your car for all your errands, get that bike out and fix it up. This makes especially good sense if the bike isn't a superlight racing machine in the first place. If it's more of a sturdy utility design than a world-class racer, why not fix it up for some more utilitarian use than gathering dust motes? You can make it as comfy as any sit-down bike, and it will be much easier to carry things on than a racy ten-speed. And the conversion will cost only about a quarter as much as getting a new ten-speed bike. It takes some time and effort, but the bike you get in the end will last for years and years.

The conversion requires changing the handlebars, stem, and brake handles on your bike; you may want to change the seat for added comfort. To make sure you get new parts that fit, it's best to take your bike to a good shop and have a reliable mechanic check the measurement of your stem diameter and the size of the steering column that it fits into.

If you can't get the bike to a good shop, you can measure the stem diameter yourself, if you have a pair of good calipers and want to order the correct size stem from a catalogue. Just make sure you order a pair of handlebars from the same catalogue, so you can be sure that *they* will fit the stem too.

In general, the stem diameters on Italian, English, and most Japanese bikes are 22.2 mm or ⁷/₈ in. Some Japanese bikes (those made for America) and all American bikes have stems that are .833 in. or ¹³/₁₆ in. in diameter. German, French, and Spanish bikes almost all have stems that are just under ⁷/₈ in. in diameter. The steering column is too small to squeeze in the standard 22.2 mm size, but a bit bigger than the American size. Bah! It's all just because each manufacturer wants you to buy *its* stem for *its* bike. We're lucky the OPEC countries haven't started producing oil that can only be used in cars made by them; that would be a pretty mess, wouldn't it? If you can't get the correct handlebars or stems, you can buy a size that's a bit smaller and use a thin metal shim to fill the gap.

The best way to make sure you get bars that fit your stem is to buy them from the same store or catalogue, and made by the same manufacturer (you have to play the game, it seems). There is a great number of different diameters of the center sections of different handlebars, so if you order from a catalogue, tell them that you want the two parts to fit together, and they will make sure the two fit, if they are decent people like the folks listed in the Addresses section at the back of this book. By the way, some nice catalogues now list an aluminum "swan" stem that is fairly tall, but that has only a 60 mm extension. This thing is obviously made for converting a ten-speed to an upright-position bike. Avoid any stem with an extension that's over 120 mm. It will force you to lean too far forward to reach the handlebars, and the bike will steer strangely, besides. It'll be sort of like trying to drive a boat that's going backward with the rudder reversed and the tiller sticking out ahead of it. Crazy, in other words.

Get new brake handles, the kind that are made for your new "allrounder" or touring-style bars. Get ferrules (end caps) for the cable housings too, if your new brake handles require new ones. If you're buying the stuff at a shop, slip a brake handle onto one end of the bar to make sure it'll fit on and tighten up completely when you turn the screw in. There are different handlebar diameters (those manufacturers don't miss a chance, do they?) and you have to get brake handles that match your bars. Once again, if you are ordering from a catalogue, order all the stuff at once, and tell them you plan to use it all on the same bike, so they'll make sure the ferrules fit the handles and the handles fit the bars.

To replace your original ten-speed equipment, first release the brakes by loosening the cable anchor bolts on the brake mechanisms (if this or any instructions that follow are unclear to you, get help from a mechanic or from a good book like *Anybody's Bike Book*). Get the little barrel- or mushroom-shaped end of each cable out of its holder in the brake handle. This takes some craning of your neck and maybe crawling

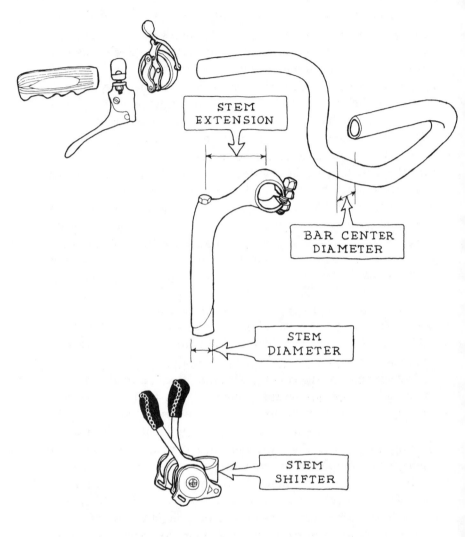

STEM
EXTENSION

BAR CENTER
DIAMETER

STEM
DIAMETER

STEM
SHIFTER

Illustration 19   Upright Conversion Parts

around under the front of the bike so you can look up inside the handle and find out what's holding the end of that cable there. If the end is resting in a U-shaped slot, monkey around with the cable and the handle, using a screwdriver or pliers, and gently slip the thing out of the slot. If the cable goes through a little hole instead of a slot, you have to pull it all the way out of the housing and the handle to get the handle loose.

When the brake cables are disengaged, check the gear-shifting levers. If you have the kind that are attached to the stem, you're in luck. Just loosen the mounting screw or bolt that holds them tight, and later you'll be able to put them right back on your new stem. If you have the tip-shifter levers that fit in the ends of the handlebars, you can take them apart, remove them by loosening (it's *clockwise* on the allen screw to loosen many of them) the allen screw inside, then tightening them onto your new bars. If you have the levers down on the down tube, you can either leave them down there, or buy a stem-shifter rig and put it onto your new stem so the levers will be up where you can reach them easier. Changing the gear levers either way will require longer cables and a little careful setting up. Have a mechanic help you, or see a good repair book to make sure you get the job done right.

To take your old handlebars off the bike, just loosen the expander bolt a couple of turns, then tap on it. Use a wrench or allen key to loosen the bolt that is at the top of the stem near the back. Tap the loosened bolt head lightly with a small hammer, using a piece of wood between the hammer and the bolt head if you don't want to harm the chrome plating. The stem will come loose in the steering column unless it's rusted tight in there. Let a penetrating oil like Liquid Wrench soak in if it's all corroded together. Pull the stem and the handlebars off the bike, leaving the brake cables and the stem shift levers (assuming you have those) dangling in the breeze. Be careful you don't bend or kink those dangling cables while you're putting the new bars in.

Put the handlebars and stem together and tighten up the stem binder bolt a bit, just to hold them in there for the time being. Push the stem through the stem-shifter unit (if you have one) and into the steering column of the bike frame. It should slide in easily, but it shouldn't be loose as a goose in there, either.

Line up the handlebars and the stem so they are pointing straight ahead when the front wheel points straight ahead. Some people can eyeball the stem and the wheel to get them lined up; others find it easier to get the handlebars perpendicular to the front wheel, so they are steering straight. Tighten the expander bolt firmly when you have things lined up by one method or the other. Leave that bolt less than supertight, though, so if you ever have an accident, the bar will twist loose if you land on the end of it. Tighten the bolt or screw that holds the stem shifter to the stem. Make sure the cables aren't twisted or stretched so they bind up when you steer from side to side.

Then sit on the bike and see if the bars are at an angle and height that's comfortable for you. Most people like them to aim down a bit at the ends. Others like the grips to be perfectly horizontal. Loosen the binder bolt and change the position of the bars if needed, then tighten the expander bolt. Make sure you use a wrench that fits well so you don't round off the head of the bolt or gouge out the hex hole if it's an allen screw.

Align the brake handles so they are easy to reach when you are in your riding position, and far enough from the ends of the handlebars that you can push the grips all the way on. Tighten the mounting screws well, but be careful you don't strip the threads; they're delicate little things.

To hook up the brake cables, pull them out of the housing if you haven't already, then cut the housings to a shorter length, so they give you enough slack to steer from side to side, but not so much that they flop all around and get in your way. Get new cables or ferrules (end caps) if you don't have ones that will fit in your new handles. When the brakes are tight enough that you have to move the end of the handle only halfway to the handlebar to fully apply the brakes, then you can push your handle grips on and your bike is ready to go.

Many people who make this conversion want to put their new handlebars up high (it's especially tempting if you have one of those swan stems), so they can be sure of getting a nice upright riding position. This does seem more comfortable at first, and it allows you to look around effortlessly, to see the city traffic or country scenery surrounding you. But it may not be too comfortable on any ride longer than a couple of miles. The more upright you sit, the more your sitzplatz smarts. And sitting on a narrow, firm racing-style saddle in that position can be especially uncomfortable.

The solution to this sort of saddle-soreness is to lower the handlebars and make sure their ends are tipped down a little, so you lean forward and rest part of your weight on your hands. The position is much less radical than the racing one, but much more comfortable than a ramrod-straight upright position, especially on longer rides. If the racing seat still feels like a 2 x 4 even after you adjust your handlebar position, get one of the more comfortable wide-style saddles, such as the classic Brooks B72, Ideale B6, or any of the wide anatomic touring saddles with the plastic foam lumps for your pelvic bones to rest on. For more info on these fancy saddles that can take all the pain out of cycling, see page 74.

You can attach carrying bags and racks to your sit-up ten-speed, as described in this chapter, or you can go to Chapter 9 and put a basket and child seat on the bike, making it into a lightweight station wagon, a sort of VW Rabbit of the bike world.

Racks, Bags, and Packs for Ten-Speeds

If you want to keep the dropped bars on your ten-speed, for the efficient, low-wind-resistance riding position, but you still need to have some way of carrying things on the bike when you go shopping around town, get the lightest and simplest carrying devices that will do the job for you.

The first step, and really a must for all cyclists, is a little cotton or nylon bike bag, also known as a rucksack, a book bag, a "trunkette", or a daypack. The lighter and simpler it is, the better. Illustration 4 shows the basic item. I like ones that are big enough to hold a beach towel and my swim fins, or maybe a half-gallon of apple juice and a dozen eggs, or a six-pack of beer. In other words, about 15 in. long by 13 or 14 in. wide. You can get a bigger rucksack, the kind hikers use for day-long outings, but these are usually too bulky to fold up and stuff in your back pocket when you aren't carrying anything. That's the beauty of the lightweight type shown on the next page. It'll carry lots of light loads, the kind you pick up every day you go downtown, but when you're riding along with no load, the pack can be tucked out of the way, and it adds hardly any weight to your bike.

Just make sure the cloth the pack is made out of is sturdy, well-sewn at the seams, and not frayed at all. And make sure the shoulder straps are of heavy nylon or cotton webbing, double-stitched at the ends. If they are sewn on at an angle, as shown, they will fit flat and comfortable against your back and sides, and they'll be stronger than straps that are sewn on horizontally.

For major shopping, the little bag is inadequate. It's good to take one on all shopping trips, but the big, roomy racks and bags that are made for the front and back of your bike should carry the bulk of your load.

Three basic rules for any load carrier are: keep it light; keep it simple; and if the load is heavy, keep it balanced. With these three rules in mind, you can add as much of the following paraphernalia to your bike as you need. Add no more than needed, though. Carriers and bags can get loose and flap around or mess up the works of your bike if you ride around with them empty all the time.

Strong Rear Rack

This doesn't mean a thing to hold up your strong, muscly behind. It means a light, sturdy rack that fits on the back of the bike in such a way that it WILL NOT COME LOOSE. You don't want anything waggling around back there, squishing down on your brakes, and generally putting your ass in a sling.

Two good examples of rear racks are shown in Illustrations 20 and 21. The first super-strong type costs about three times more than the economy type, but it is much lighter and yet stronger. If you have a light bike and are willing to shell out some extra money to keep it light, go for this model. The one shown is made by Jim Blackburn, but there are others that do

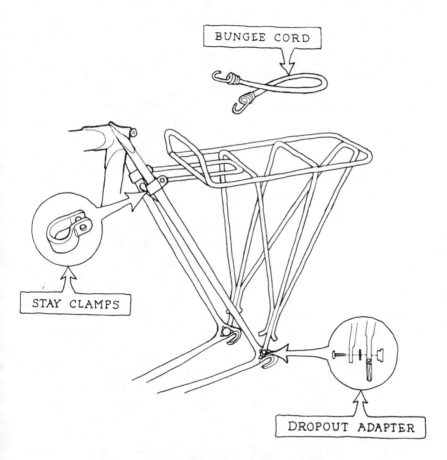

Illustration **20**   Super-strong Rack

pretty much the same job. They are designed to fit little brazed-on eyelets on the seat stays, and protruding eyelets on the top of the rear drop-outs above the wheel axle. But if your bike doesn't have those eyelets, you can get stay clamps and special bolts, nuts, and washers to fit the triangular hole found in the drop-out on most touring and racing bikes. These attachment gizmos are made by Blackburn, and they can be bought from good touring shops or from the better catalogues (see Addresses). If you need seat stay clamps, make sure you get ones for the diameter of seat stay you have. Measure the width of the stay at the point the clamp tightens around, then get that size clamp (it'll probably be $9/16$-inch or $5/8$-inch on a big heavy-duty bike, or maybe $1/2$-inch if it's an oddball delicate bike). Be cautious but firm when you tighten up all the little bolts and nuts so they'll stay tight and keep the rack rigid. If it's hard to get the bolts, nuts, and washers into place on the drop-outs, just take the rear wheel off the bike to give yourself some working space. If you can't get the rack level, you can bend the two bars that go to the seat stays, but do it SLOWLY and GENTLY, using either a small pipe over each bar, or putting both bars in a vice with padded jaws. Do not make any sharp bends or you'll weaken the aluminum; instead, bend a bit at a time, then move your bending device toward the end of the bar after each bend, so you make a nice smooth curve.

The second rack, shown in Illustration 21, is much cheaper, but there are models that are fairly well made, although heavier than the Blackburn. Make *sure* you get a little support plate if you choose to make do with an inexpensive rack and want to carry lots of groceries and stuff on it. The plate may look like the one shown, or it may be more of a triangle, or a rectangle with a row of holes in it. Any of the standard support plates will work with the Pletscher rack. If you don't use some support, though, the front end of your rack will work loose sooner or later and slide down on the brake mechanism, pushing it cockeyed so one brake shoe drags, or squeezing the cables so the back brakes stay on all the time. This will slow you down something awful.

So get that support plate, and when you put the rack on your bike, put the bolts through the bottom holes on the long

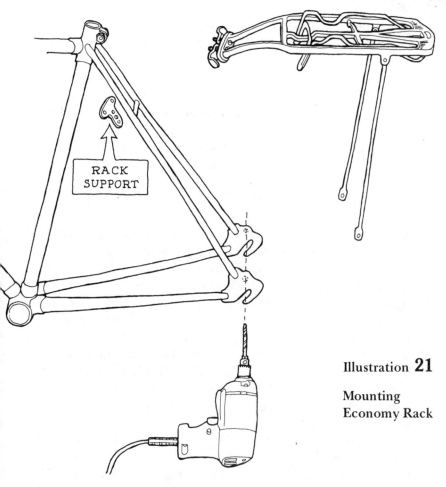

RACK
SUPPORT

Illustration **21**

Mounting
Economy Rack

skinny rack braces and attach them to the dropouts on the bike *before* you attach the front end of the rack to the seat stays. If you don't have eyelets for the brace bolts, look and see if your dropouts are the racy kind with a little triangular hole, as shown in Illustration 20. Get Blackburn mounting bolts and washers if that's the case. If you have flat-plate metal dropouts, use a high-speed drill and a $^3/_{16}$-inch bit to cut a hole for the bolt. If you have any trouble fitting the bolts and nuts into the dropouts, remove the rear wheel of the bike to give yourself some clear working space.

Don't tighten the mounting bolts to the dropout yet; you have to line up the rack so it's flat first. Put the rear wheel back on the bike if you removed it.

Now you can mount the support plate. If the plate has grooves in it, make sure it is set with the grooves meshed against the stays. Take the nut (and the flat washer, if there is one) off the brake bolt, push the bolt through the bottom hole in the support plate, then tighten the nut back on, holding the brake straight as you do so. Now put the bolts through the rack holes and the holes in the plate that are lined up with them when the rack is level. Tighten the nuts on, then go back down to the bottoms of the braces and tighten up those bolts and nuts too. Make sure all of the nuts are good and tight, but don't twist so hard on them you strip the threads. You can use a thread adhesive like Loctite for added strength on those bolts and nuts.

So, you now have a nice solid rack. How do you hold things on it? You use bungee cords. These elastic cords, with hooks on the ends, are also known as tie-downs, Sandow cords, shock cords, or stretch cords. They work well no matter what name you stretch to fit them. If you are carrying something that makes a neat bundle all by itself, like a notebook and two textbooks, or a sleeping bag, or a tennis racket, all you have to do is put the object or objects on the rack in such a way that they don't stick out too far on the sides, then hook one end of a bungee on the rack and wrap it around your load and the rack, using the cord to press the load up against the front corner of the rack. Most good racks are turned up at the front for that purpose. Keep the cord as tight as possible until you hook the other end to the rack frame, and avoid running the cord between the rack and the tire, where it might get worn away. Test the tie-down by shaking the bike and bouncing it up and down vigorously a few times. If the load stays firm and in place, you can ride off with confidence.

If you have to carry a more fragile or ungainly load, like three heads of loose-leaf lettuce and a loaf of bread, or a tinker-toy contraption your proud child wants to convey to a friend's house without bending it or dismantling ONE SINGLE PIECE, then you have to use some kind of container on your sturdy rack. The two best choices are a sturdy cardboard case that had bottles in it, or a heavier but handier wicker basket.

Cardboard cases that are made to carry bottles of expensive liquid such as booze or imported jams and jellies are often made of double-weight cardboard, with holes for the handles.

There are some sturdy fruit cartons like this, too. The best size is about ten inches wide by fourteen inches long by a foot high. You can easily set the box crosswise on the rack and hold it there with two bungee cords, as the basket is held in Illustration 22. If the top flaps of the box haven't been cut off, fold and tape them down inside. This will increase the life span of the box greatly.

Illustration **22**   **Basket Secure With Bungee Cords**

People have carried their vittles home from the garden or the market in nice little cane or wicker baskets for centuries. A basket may be heavier, but it will last longer if you're careful with it; it's also easier to use and more aesthetic.

One problem with either the box or the basket is that they are too small to hold more than one normal-size shopping bag. If you get a box that's big enough to hold two shopping bags, though, it will be too big for your rear rack.

The solution is simple and radical. Don't use shopping bags. Carry your basket or box right into the store and fill it directly off the shelves. That way you'll be sure not to buy more than you can carry. If you *have* to get a little more than will fit, you should have your light bike bag in your pocket to carry the excess home on your back.

Shopping by the basket seems like a pain at first. You have to limit yourself to small amounts, and you have to go back to the store quite often. But over the years, as we have done our shopping this way, we have become more and more attached to the method, and we even feel it saves us money, because we don't buy big packages of prepared food, but rather find the bulk items that we can pack more easily; these are either grains, meats, vegetables, or fruits. If they are fresh and in season, they cost less than the prepared foods.

For instance, you can't buy many big boxes of breakfast cereal if you want to carry them on a bike. The high price of small boxes of cereal makes them prohibitive, too. So you buy some things in bulk, like rolled oats, sunflower seeds, coconut chips, and honey, and you make your own granola. And it tastes a hundred times better than any sugar-coated stuff out of a flashy box. You buy five pounds of flour instead of five loaves of bread. You steer clear of tinfoil TV dinners, fluffy angel cakes, and potato chips in puffy bags. You tend to buy less air and more substance, in other words. And even when you buy produce, you tend to get better, riper stuff, because you know you'll be back to the store before long, so there's no point in buying rock-hard green fruits and vegetables so they can ripen later at home.

This whole scheme of shopping in small amounts on a bicycle is hard if you live miles from the nearest store. For country people, the big bicycle station wagon makes more sense (see page 87). For most urban and suburban dwellers, though, the ten-speed with a good rear rack and box or basket will do you fine, and give you plenty of chances for good exercise going to and from the store.

Handlebar Pack

If you want a closed carrying device on your bike, so you can drop small purchases or things like your lunch sack into it, instead of having to strap them onto a rear rack, you can get a handy pack that goes between your drop handlebars. They come in a wide variety of sizes, styles, and prices, so you should shop around before you buy one, and make sure you get a pack that is light but strong enough for your purposes. It should have a main compartment that's big enough for the things you'll carry most often, but it should still fit between your bars and leave enough room for your hands, no matter which riding position you're using. On a long ride it will drive you nuts if your hands bump against an oversize pack. Take your bike to the shop and mount the pack and its support on your own bars before you buy it. There's no substitute for actually trying the thing out to make sure it fits.

MAPCASE

Illustration **23**

Touring Handlebar Pack

Some good points to look for on any pack are a simple mounting support and bungee cords that go down to the fork ends as shown. The cord hooks can be fixed up as described on page 15 if you don't have eyelets on those dropouts. If you plan to tour a lot, you may want front, side, and top pockets on your bag, with a see-through map case on top of the whole outfit. For shopping and local commuting, though, it's better to get a pack with one big, deep compartment that you can load and unload easily.

The largest packs hold up to 600 cubic inches. If you're getting the kind with just one main compartment, try to find one that holds at least 300 cubic inches. This will take a half-gallon carton of milk and a dozen eggs, along with some smaller stuff.

Avoid handlebar packs that have heavy mounting bars that curve all over the place, or supports that only hold the pack loosely, and don't have any bungee cords to hold the bottoms down tight. Some packs have crummy zippers that tend to jam or come apart, and other packs have zippers that don't open wide enough to get things in and out easily. Steer clear of these models, too.

Panniers and Other Rear-End Packs

These packs mount on either a strong rear rack (see page 57) or on the back of the bike's saddle. For mini-loads, use a seat pack like the one shown in Illustration 6. Get one with adequate webbing or an internal frame so it won't sag all the way down and rub on the back wheel, and make sure the zipper or top flap opens wide enough to get things in and out easily. The biggest bother to me about seat packs is that they waggle back and forth and scrape against the backs of your thighs every time you extend your legs while pedaling. The best seat packs are carefully designed so they are held firmly to the seat post, without being pulled forward on their loops so they hit your legs. Any seat pack will bump your legs if your seat doesn't have those loops to hang it from. To put nice loops on your racing or touring saddle, see the homemade bar on page 14, or get the ready-made loops they have in catalogues (see Addresses). For racers who have sew-ups, there's another trick to hold a saggy seat pack up and away from your legs. Put a spare tire clamp for a sew-up on the seat rails and hook the pack straps around the rails *above* the tire clamp. If you use sew-ups, you can even fold up a tire and mount the pack behind it, with the straps that attach to the seat post stretched around that tire, too. It's harder to get to your spare when you have a flat, but to me the comfort of keeping the pack back where it can't hit my legs is worth the trouble.

Take your bike to the store when you are looking at seat packs so you can be sure to get one that fits well. If the thing isn't going to be snug in there and yet stay clear of your legs, forget it.

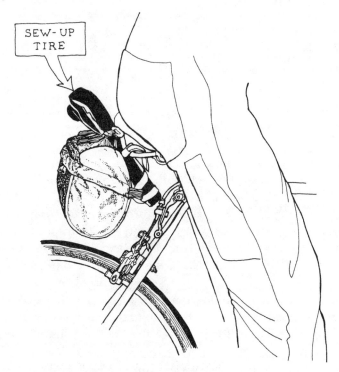

SEW-UP
TIRE

Illustration 24 A   Seat Pack Kept Clear of Legs

If you have a sturdy rear rack and need to carry small- to medium-size loads, you can buy a handy rack pack that fits on top of your rack. These are light, easy to use, and very durable if they're made out of good materials. The best ones have some

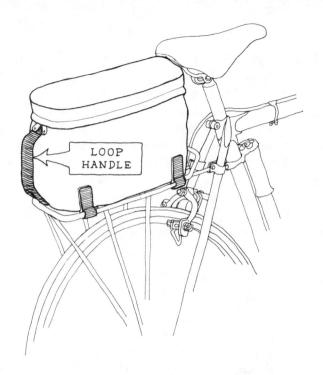

LOOP
HANDLE

Illustration **24**B   Rack Pack

kind of internal stiffener, a loop handle, and straps that bind firmly to the rack so the pack can't slop around at all.

Finally, for great big loads, there are panniers. I wouldn't use these unless I didn't have any other choice. They are certainly a good way to carry lots of stuff on a ten-speed, if they are well-supported by a good rack like the one in Illustration 20, but if you put all of your load in them and none on the front of the bike, you will have a real tail-wagging problem. For touring they can be used in combination with a large handlebar pack for a more balanced load, and this combination can also be used for large shopping loads. But it makes the bike ride like a truck. If you have money and room enough to store two bikes, it will be better to get a station wagon three-speed (see page 87) for your heavy local shopping and leave your ten-speed unencumbered so you can have more fun on longer rides. One viable compromise is to use a slide-mounting pannier and rack system, such as the unit made by Eclipse. This will allow you to get the panniers on and off with ease, so you can have a light, sporty bike until you need all the load-carrying capacity of the panniers.

Techniques

There are simple methods of shopping on a bike that will make the most of the equipment described in this chapter. First, keep good shopping lists. If you live within three miles of the stores where you do most of your shopping, and you don't have to go through too much traffic to get there, it'll be OK to make about two shopping trips a week. If your shopping lists are good, you won't have to ride back to the store every day to get single items you forgot. You might even keep two lists, one in the kitchen for foodstuffs, and one in your wallet or purse for things you remember when you're at work.

Keep your load-carrying devices right near your bicycle. We have our little bike bags hanging on a hook by the back door. If you use a wicker basket, hang it on a hook right by the bike; keep your leg light in the same place, too, so you'll remember to take it if you're going to be out after dark.

Learn to buy bulk goods instead of prepared foods in gaudy packages, as outlined in the basket shopping method on page 62.

Learn to get the best products that are available locally. This is a sacrilege against the religion of jump-in-the-car bargain hunting. But to me it implies a return to a more friendly way of shopping. You get to know the local markets and shops that have things that suit your tastes, then you make an effort to befriend the proprietors and inform them carefully of your tastes, so you can work *with* them to get the things you like at as low a price as possible. For produce, the ideal situation for this sort of village shopping attitude is the farmers' market. This doesn't necessarily mean a country market; one of the best farmers' markets in the world is in Brooklyn, New York. But if you aren't lucky enough to have a farmers' market within cycling distance, you can develop a good relationship with your local grocer, butcher, and shopkeepers, even if they are in super-markets, department stores, or shopping malls. The essence of the thing is that you do *not* roam around looking for bargains, but rather develop a strong sense of what you want and get it close to home.

Let the shopkeepers find the bargains and tell you about them. Of course, the old rule of "let the buyer beware" still holds true, and you have to watch for things like loss leaders and supposed bargains that are really just crummy products the shopkeeper wants to unload on you. But if you do build up a solid understanding with a good grocer or shopkeeper, you won't have to read *Consumer Reports* to check up on the person all the time. A good shopkeeper who knows you well will get the best for you and steer you away from things he or she knows you won't like. If not, the shopkeeper knows that he or she may lose a good regular customer.

If you shop at only a few stores, you can work out things like how to get to them without fighting too much traffic, and how to park in a safe place that's out-of-the-way yet near the store. To get the bike in and out of narrow parking areas, swing the front end up and use the upright walk-along trick shown in Illustration 18.

A great new gizmo has been invented to help you lean the bike in precarious places where it might tend to roll and flop over. The Flickstand, which costs only a few bucks and adds almost no weight to the bike, is a much more efficient parking aid than the standard kickstand.

To mount the Flickstand, first wrap its plastic body around your down tube where it is near the curve of the front wheel. Make sure none of the cables are caught under the body of the Flickstand. If the ends of the thing wrap all the way around and touch each other so it's loose, you have a smaller than normal down tube; put the flat shim of plastic under the Flickstand body so it'll fit right. See that the little grooves in the plastic run forward from the hole in it, then squeeze the body tight around the down tube, pick up the wire loop, stretch the ends apart, and pop them into the small holes so the round curve is sticking down and toward the back of the bike, as shown in Illustration 25A. There will probably be a short and a long wire piece to choose from. The longer one is for bikes that have more than 1⅝ inches of space between the tire and the down tube at the closest point. The short one is for those sporty and racy bikes that have less than 1⅝ inches of space. If there is too much space for even the long wire loop to reach the tire, bend the curved tire-hitting section of the longer loop so it sticks down farther. This will give you enough reach for almost any bike.

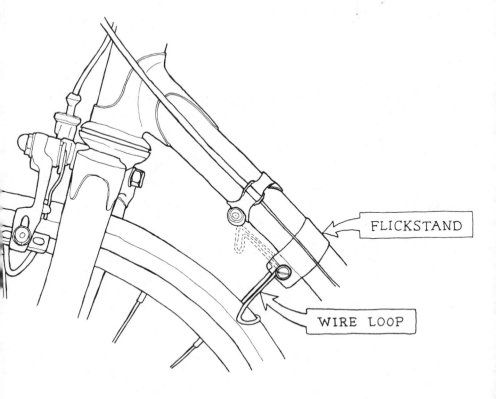

FLICKSTAND

WIRE LOOP

Illustration **25** A   Flickstand

When your chosen wire piece is in place, turn the front wheel so it is steering to one side, then slide the Flickstand up and down the tube until it is at the point where the frame is closest to the curve of the tire. Keep the tire steered to the side for now, so you don't have to actually push the wire against it. See if you can fold the wire up and down without hitting your gear changer levers, a pump bracket, or the cable housing brackets. If any of those things are in the way, take the wire off, turn the Flickstand body around, and put the wire back on with the curve sticking up and toward the front of the bike, the opposite of how it is in Illustration 25A. The Flickstand will hold this way as long as you don't park the bike pointing up a steep hill with a heavy load.

Put the little bolt through the washer, then through the plastic body. Spin the nut on with your fingers, but don't

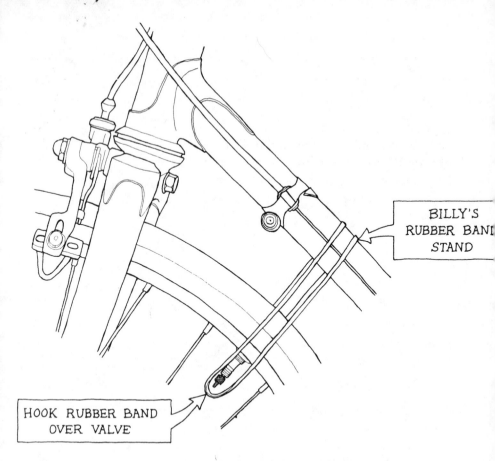

BILLY'S
RUBBER BAND
STAND

HOOK RUBBER BAND
OVER VALVE

Illustration 25B   Rubber Band Stand

tighten the thing yet. Leave it loose enough to slide the body around on the tube to position it in such a place that the wire goes straight down and dimples the tire when the wheel is steering straight and the wire is locked in its down position. This takes some fooling around with the wire, flicking it up and locking it down. The wire should dimple the tire in when it's locked down, but it should be easy to flick up when you want to ride the bike away. Screw the bolt tight when everything is set just right. If the wire is loose, or gets loose with time, so it doesn't stay up like it should when not in use, take the Flickstand apart and push the ends of the wire together or even past each other, so when you let go of them the ends still touch. Then you can put the thing back together and the wire will flick up and down and stay where you put it.

If you can't find the Flickstand at your local bike shop, you can order one from a catalogue (see Addresses). Or you can use a homemade rubber-band stand to do the same job. Billy Menchine showed me how to stretch a rubber band from your valve stem up around the down tube and back to the valve stem. It works OK, and you can put the rubber band around your brake lever post when it isn't in use, but it isn't quite so convenient or as snazzy as the Flickstand. That little metal-and-plastic unit is an irresistable bit of Yankee ingenuity—a great example of a useful adult toy.

Chapter 7
Vacationing on a Ten-Speed

DON'T GIVE up your tour of the nearest mountain region, or your holiday along the coast, just because gas is scarce. If you are the stalwart and self-sufficient type, you can just load up the bike with a handlebar pack, seat pack, and rack pack, then set off on your own. Or if you like to travel light, you can join a group and do a tour with a "sagwagon" that matches your route, carries the luggage, picks up stragglers, and uses only a fraction of the gas you'd use if you all drove. If you travel to a camp or rental place near a beach, you can take a bike along and use it to get from your sleeping place to the water, thus saving gas and getting more exercise on your holiday.

For any sort of vacation use, your bike should be a good light one, and yet very durable, so you can spend your vacation time having fun instead of fiddling with a broken bicycle. The most crucial elements of the machine in this respect are the frame and wheels. The frame can be anything from a standard mass-produced lugged model made by one of the big companies to an elegant custom model with fancy refinements for touring. If the tubes are made from high-carbon or chrome molybdenum steel, and seamless, and if they are joined carefully, they will probably be light and strong enough to do the job. The tubes do not have to be butted. I have ridden a number of production bikes with straight-gauge tubes that were quite responsive and plenty strong enough for touring. On the other hand, I've come across bikes with butted tubing that were so sloppily brazed together I could see gaps between the lugs and the tubes, evidence of dangerous weakness at those points. So shop carefully for a bike you intend to tour on, but don't feel that you have to spend your life savings on the thing. If you get a good older frame and fix up the other components so they're reliable, you can have a great touring machine for about a quarter the cost of a new custom-made one.

On any frame you are considering, look for seat and head-set angles of about 72 degrees, and a long (over 104 cm or 41 in.) wheelbase. Look at Illustration 45 to get an idea of what those dimensions are. Or you can eyeball the frame to see how close the rear wheel is to the seat tube and how close the front wheel is to the down tube. Compare a hotshot criterium racing bike and a fancy touring model, and you'll see the difference right away. The touring bike has a more laid-back, spread-out look. It's nice to have a tapered-gauge fork on your touring bike, too, one that has at least two-and-a-quarter inches or 55 mm of forward rake. This kind of fork will absorb lots of road shocks, even when the bike is heavily loaded, and it will keep you much more comfortable than a stiff fork will on a long day of bumpy riding. Make sure there are eyelets on the fork ends and on the rear drop-outs for your pack racks (see page 58).

The wheels, especially the rear one, should be strong. If you weigh over 175 pounds, you may even want a custom-made 40-spoke wheel with heavy-duty 14-gauge rustless spokes and a strong aluminum alloy or even a steel rim. Get the highest quality and strength money can buy, whichever rim you choose. You can plan on having some flats on your rear tire if you are heavy and carrying a heavy load on a tour, so get good clincher tires such as the Specialized Bicycle Imports Touring models. They are made with strong, light materials and have a long-wearing center ridge and the capability to carry pressures up to 90 pounds. Even if you do have flat problems, I don't recommend using airless tires (as in Illustrations 15 and 16). They give too rough a ride for long-distance riding. If you have sturdy sew-up wheels and you and your load aren't going to add up to more weight than about 175 pounds, you can use strong, large-diameter tubular tires like the famous Clement Campionato del Mundo ("World Champion"). If the del Mundo is too pricy, try the new nylon or polyester cord sew-ups, which are made to be as sturdy and light as the del Mundo, but which cost less.

Don't get a rear wheel with a superthin lightweight rim and a narrow profile tire. You need a little more width for strength in the rim, and the wider profile of the tires that fit the bigger rims will help your bike absorb the shocks of chuckholes and rocks, even when you are riding down a big hill with 30 pounds of gear on your rear rack.

All other equipment on the bike should be reasonably light, but don't get space-age titanium stuff. There's no way you can save enough grams on it to make up for the pounds of clothes and gear you're going to be carrying. Instead, concentrate on convenience and comfort. Get a good solid chain like the Sedis, which will last and fit all standard freewheels. It will cost you about a tenth as much as a titanium chain.

Get a handlebar and stem set that are completely comfortable for your reach, neither too long, nor too wide, nor too narrow, nor too deep, nor too shallow. You'll be most happy on the road if your bars are set so you can ride in a number of different positions, like with your hands on the tops of the bars, along the sides, on the brake posts, or on the lower portion. Tape the bars thoroughly with at least two layers of good cotton tape such as Tressostar, or plastic tape if you prefer that slick, clean feel. There are thick tubes of handlebar padding you can use if your hands ache or go numb from the pounding they get on long rides. They give you a squishy-wishy sense of control, though. This may not be worth the extra hand protection.

Get a seat that fits you very well and that is made for long rides. This doesn't mean a triple-padded fleece-coated wide-ass motorcycle-type seat. Leave those for the Harley hogs. A good seat for touring will be narrow where it sticks between your thighs so the thighs won't rub and chafe on it. Even if it has some padding where your two pelvic bones rest, that padding should be held on a firm leather or nylon base. The saddle should not be cushy, in other words. If you have lots of trouble breaking in a hard new leather saddle you may want to try one of the newer plastic touring seats with two padded bulges placed where your bones rest. These don't feel that great to me, but some riders swear by them. Avocet and Selle Milano make

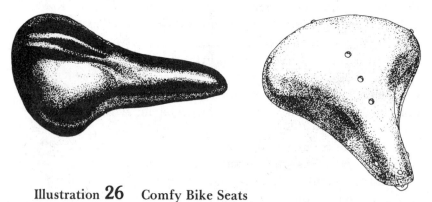

Illustration 26   **Comfy Bike Seats**

fine examples in the anatomic design. There are also saddles made especially for women, such as the Avocet women's models, and the Ideale B6, which is a masterpiece of leatherwork, up in the same range of quality as the Brooks touring saddles.

All leather bike seats take some getting used to. Before a tour, ride on yours a number of times (say on at least five two-hour rides) and use some mink oil on it so it gets little soft places where your hard pelvic bones push into it. Once you and your saddle fit together well, you'll be able to use it in comfort for years.

To carry baggage on your tour, get a strong rack for the rear of your bike (see page 5 7) and a little backpack or a roomy roomy handlebar pack. Then see how small and light you can keep your load. If possible, avoid getting those big panniers.

That sounds like blasphemy. What?! Touring on a bike without panniers? How could I suggest such a thing? The reason is simple. The bigger your bags, the more junk you'll take on your tour. You always think each item you're putting in will help make life more comfortable out on the road. But in total, all the stuff makes your tour LESS comfortable because it turns your bike into an RV with handling characteristics like an over-loaded Winnebago. And the reason you've chosen cycle touring is to get *away* from the sort of quantity-over-quality syndrome represented by a gas-swilling motor home.

Here's how to get by with less. PLAN your trip well and SAVE some money so you can make a number of stops along the way at restaurants, motels, youth hostels (see AYH in Addresses), and friends' houses (always leave a gift). Don't go

full-on camping, especially in areas where there's lots of rain. For short showers, you can get by with a light plastic poncho and a lot of hiding under the eaves of barns and country stores. If you try to carry camping gear and rain outfits that keep you prepared for every typhoon, hailstorm, and tornado, you'll fill your panniers to bursting and your weight load will be horrific. If you have to camp along your route, do it with the lightest bare minimum of equipment, like the stuff mountain climbers use. Tour in relatively warm country and you can use a light sleeping bag that doesn't have all the filler necessary for comfort at minus-fifteen degrees Fahrenheit. Light and miniature equipment is expensive. If you can borrow some of it you'll save lots of money. But don't take heavy gear if you can possibly avoid it.

I carry less than 15 pounds of gear on my tours. I have an 8-by-16-inch stuffsack that goes on my rear rack. In it goes a light-duty sleeping bag (comfortable to 20 degrees F) and my spare socks, undershirts, cycling shorts, and swimming trunks (nylon racing ones that are really minimal). There's a little nylon windbreaker folded up in there, and a plastic bag with toiletries and some tiny things that can make a big comfort difference, like dark glasses for glare, Cutter's repellent for insects, sunscreen and lip balm for hot days, and a pocket knife for all the millions of jobs it can do.

Under my seat I have a little nylon bag (called a B/C bag). Inside it are a mini-patch kit, a spare inner tube, a sawed-off crescent wrench, a screwdriver, and two tire irons (aluminum, no less). On my back I carry my faithful cloth pack with maps, long pants (cords if it's cool, seersuckers if it's hot) to wear in restaurants, and my sweater for cool mornings. A banana and some raisins or even a sandwich can be stuffed in there too. I wear cotton T-shirts, and a flannel shirt if it's cool. These garments don't look as racy as wool jerseys, but they are easier to wash and dry, and more acceptable in country cafes and roadstops. If you want to avoid the stares and catcalls the black wool shorts attract, you can go one step farther and wear nice brown cotton/polyester ones like those sold by Bikecology (see Addresses).

I wear a helmet if I'm riding in traffic. Out in the country I wear a terrycloth sailor's cap that's really handy; it can be washed and dried on the run, or even left wet on your head to keep you cool. It looks a bit Gabby Hayes-like when I fold the front up for a downhill sprint, but funny looks are of much less concern to me than comfort on the road. I can fold it up and put it in my pack when I go into a restaurant.

The other way to keep your bike's weight down on tour is to ride with a group and use a sagwagon—a single car that carries the suitcases and sleeping bags for the whole group. If the idea of using a lot of gas for a big panel truck or station wagon is unappealing to you, start the tour from right at home (so you don't have to transport all the bikes and riders to the beginning point) and use a little car with a bike rack on top for picking up an occasional straggler; load all your gear inside, leaving room for the driver and straggler only. The only problem with this approach is that if major storms or some injuries wipe out a large portion of the touring group on any one day, the little car may have to make a lot of trips in order to bring all the lost sheep back to the fold. But with good plans and a little luck, you can get along fine with a mini-sagwagon. Before you leave on tour, make sure all the riders are up to the route, make sure the bikes are in good shape, and include time for bad weather in your plan if you live in an area where you're liable to run into storms.

The point is that you can enjoy your lightweight ten-speed on long trips in a number of ways without having to load it down like a pack mule. If you really want to pack all your worldly possessions onto a bike and take a long, leisurely ramble with no plan or goal, this is fine, too; it's a great way to see the world for pennies. According to an old Chinese saying, it's bad to travel fast because it's like trying to see "flowers from horseback". But for slow, loaded-down life on the road, the best bike is the three-speed station wagon (see page 87) with a sturdy rack on the back and panniers, as well as the big basket on the front. This vehicle isn't very spry and sporty, but it can take you, at a nice flower-watching speed, over all kinds of terrain, over all the continents of the earth. You will have very little mechanical trouble with it, and you'll be able to find parts almost anywhere you wander. I could tell you a story, for instance, of riding a Schwinn Typhoon over one of the highest passes in the Andes. Ah, what a view! And what a workout!

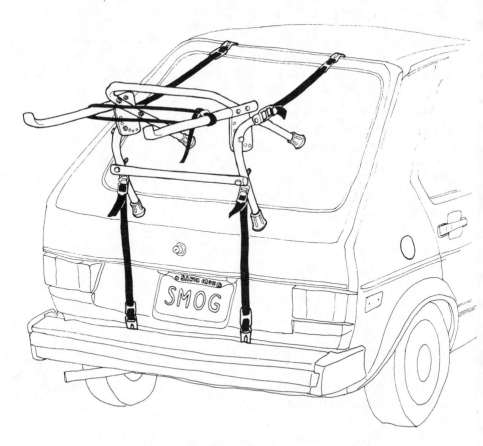

Illustration 27   **Adjustable Bike Carrier**

You can take your bike on vacations even if you don't like long-range rambles around the countryside. When you take the kind of vacation for which you pile all your luggage and kiddies into the car and drive to the nearest beach or lake, you will camp in a tent or stay in a rented cottage. Take your bike along for short rides down to the waterfront or to stores that are near your summer house or campsite.

To take the bike on your car, you can put it on a roof rack or on a rack that fits the back of your car, like the nifty Adjusta-porter. Attach the bike firmly to either kind of rack, and make sure the whole unit is tight on the car before you get out on the freeway and subject the bike and rack to 60 mph winds. We use old inner tubes to tie our bikes on our roof rack. Cut through each tube in one place, then tie one end to the rack and wrap the rest of it around the joints of bike and rack, cinch it down supertight. Tie the other end of the tube down when you've used it all up. The tube won't come loose like a rope, and it's quick and easy to undo at the trip's end.

When you arrive at your vacation spot, you can take a short ride right away to see the local sights, learn where things are in the neighborhood, and get your bearings in general. This is such a treat when you've picked a mountain or seaside spot with nice clean air! And the little introductory ride can save you lots of time later on, when you'll be able to go right to the spots you want without looking all over for them. If you stay to the side of the road and out of traffic, you can go slow and not bother the locals by being a Sunday driver. You'll find that you get to know the locals much more quickly on a bike, too.

For grocery trips and riding down to the beach or lake, you'll need either a sturdy rack (see page 57) or a roomy backpack, or both. It's best to have packs that can be carried easily *off* the bike, because you often want to take trail hikes, or park your bike and carry your beach gear across the sand to the water's edge.

Leaving a ten-speed parked by the beach can be a high-risk situation, so you'll need a good chain to lock both the wheels and the frame to a post. We have found a great beach near where we live, one that has a jetty running out to the water. We ride or walk the bikes out the jetty to our swimming place, then leave them right there where we can keep an eye on them. If you can use a similar method on a pier, boardwalk, or even a rocky promontory that runs out to the water near where you like to swim, you can keep your bike within sight. Don't take the bike out onto the beach, though. Sand and ten-speeds don't mix well. In fact, they have a grating relationship, and the sand always wins out in the long run.

There are good alternatives to using a ten-speed at your vacation site. Many tourist areas have bike rentals, where you can pick up a one-speed balloon-tire bike, or a funky three-speed for a low weekly rate. As long as there aren't any big hills around, you'll be able to take nice shorter rides on such a machine. You can put large bags in the basket if it has one (they often do), or you can wear a backpack and ride comfortably in the upright position. In fact, if you have both a ten-speed and a three-speed station wagon at home, it will make more sense to take the three-speed to your vacation spot, unless you plan to do extensive rides instead of lots of short runs to the beach or store, carrying packages and gear.

To me, the three-speed is the perfect machine for the whole feeling of being on vacation. You ride it slowly as you meander around your vacation spot, and you can observe and enjoy all the landscape and natural beauty when you're sitting up on that kind of bike. Also, you are sitting up where you can look around at traffic well. Vacation spots almost always have narrow streets with congested traffic, and if you're on a three-speed you'll be able to ride more effectively in the slow-moving crowd.

Chapter 8
Riding a Ten-Speed in Rough Weather

RIDING IN rain is a nightmare. Water falls up instead of down. Little puddles turn into bottomless peatbogs. Smooth highways turn into oil slicks, and downhill runs become exercises in brakeless, breakneck madness. It would all make your hair stand on end if your hair wasn't sopping and stuck to your freezing forehead.

Avoid riding a ten-speed in heavy rain or snow. Take the bus to work or get in a car pool for any commuting trips you have to do during full-on storms. Use a car or even a taxi to do your shopping, or walk with an umbrella when you need to get things close to home. Don't try to do EVERY trip on your bicycle. There is a point at which it is better to compromise with the more energy-intensive modes of transportation and leave your bike at home, out of the elements.

But for those of you who are devoted to getting around on a bike, to the point where you don't have a backup transit mode ready every time the skies change their mood (and in many places, the skies can be treacherously moody), there will be times when you are caught off guard, when you have to use the bike, even if you don't want to. In cases of critical fuel shortages, which seem almost inevitable these days, you may be stuck with no alternative, even if you have a car on hand. This chapter gives you a bunch of ideas for equipment alternatives and techniques you can use to make your rough-weather cycling tolerable, if not pleasant.

The first thing you can do to your bike to prepare it for stormy weather is to put fenders and a seat cover on it. These items cost only about as much as a new tire and tube, and they make a huge difference in how wet you get if you are cycling just after a rain or even during light rainfall. They will not keep you dry in a downpour, but they do help even in that nasty situation.

The better fenders, such as the Bleumels plastic type shown in Illustration 28, weigh less than one pound and provide excellent protection from water splashing up from your tires. They mount on the brake mounting bolts and on eyelets attached to your dropouts. If your bike doesn't have those dropout eyelets, you may still be able to put on a rear fender if your frame has little triangular holes in the rear dropouts. Put a Blackburn dropout bolt (see Illustration 20) in that triangular hole, and mount the struts on that bolt. With just a rear fender, you can ride straight and slow, and the only things that'll get splattered much by the front wheel are the toes of your shoes. In heavy rain more water will splash up, but you need a full weatherproof suit to keep dry in that kind of weather anyway.

When mounting fenders like the ones shown, first attach the little metal tab to the brake bolt; on the rear fender, attach the front end of the fender to the short tube between the chainstays of the frame. Then put the ends of the struts or braces through the small clamp screws on the edges of the fender and tighten those screws with your fingers until they barely pinch the struts. Line up the loop end of each strut with the dropout eyelet (on the new models both struts on each side come to the same loop, so you have only one loop to line up with each eyelet). To get the loops aligned, slide the ends of the struts in and out through the clamp screws. When all the loops are lined up, bolt them tightly to the eyelets. Do a little more scooching up and down of the clamp screws to get the fender aligned with the wheel. It should be about half an inch above the tread, and the tire should be centered between the struts so that even if you pick up a little mud on the tire, it won't hit the fender.

If you have to ride through some nasty, sticky, gumbo-type mud (we seem to specialize in that type here in central California), try to scrape it off with a stick or ride through a puddle to loosen and wash it off, before it builds into a big clot between the fender and the tire. Clots tend to form in the area behind the brakes and the area between the chainstays. They can bend or break the fender or freeze up the brakes, so keep an eye out for them and clean them out before they build up too much.

If you have to ride in ice and snow, you can get tire studs similar to those used by cars (see I. P. Limhike in Addresses) or you can order snow chains from the catalogues. Although they don't give you great traction, and although they can get broken if you're rough with them, the chains and the studs can help in certain types of snowy conditions.

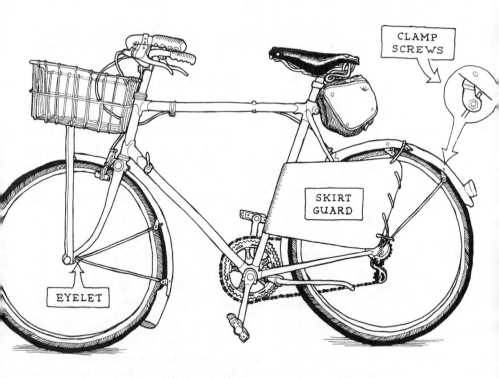

Illustration **28**   Equipped for Wet Weather

If you are a woman, or a Scots Highlander, or a transvestite (a person can't be sexist about these matters) and you want to keep your skirt or kilt out of the muddy, wet rear wheel, you can use a shield like the one shown in Illustration 28. Sad to say, the bike shops and catalogues are so anti-skirtist (or anti-kiltist) they don't sell skirt/kilt guards anymore, other than as part of a baby seat. Sometimes *I* wear *my* kilt when I'm not taking one of the kids out on the bike; I think it's an outrage that I can't get a kilt guard for my bike without buying a whole child seat!

Like so many other problems in the era of limits, this one can be solved only if you are willing to do a little work yourself. The liberating procedure is to get a piece of heavy (at least 6 mil) plastic and cut a diamond shape out of it that will cover the rear frame triangle. Punch holes around the edges with a paper punch, stretch the plastic tight, and lace it into place with shoelaces, as shown in Illustration 28.

If you have a leather saddle and have to ride much in the rain, make sure you have a seat cover as well as a good coating of leather-curing oil, such as Brooks Proofhide, on your seat. The seat cover is just a modified bathing cap made to fit the shape of your seat. There are several different makes, each with slightly different material and a slightly different shape. Find the seat cover that best fits your own seat and the bike's seat. If you use fenders, the seat cover, and an adequate poncho, and if you don't ride too fast through big puddles, you may be able to keep your crotch dry. Whenever your crotch does get wet, though, try to get someplace where you can change to dry clothes before you go on riding. If you keep pedaling for any distance you'll get major rashes and sores on your sitzplatz.

When you have no choice but to ride in the rain and mist a lot—like, if you live in Eugene, Oregon, or around the Okefenokee Swamp—you should get a poncho that's made specifically for cycling, and maybe even some chaps to keep your legs dry, and you should put stretchy waterproof booties over your feet. The best ponchos, like the one made by Eclipse, are urethane-coated nylon with a snug-fitting hood that can be drawn close around your face without impeding your vision too much. These ponchos have finger and leg loops that keep them from flapping all over the place in the wind, and they are lightweight so you can fold them up and tuck them into your pack when it stops raining. They look screamingly funny when you get off your bike and walk around with them on (you appear to be a circus tent out for a stroll), but they'll keep you quite dry while riding.

Ponchos cost a bundle. They are about the same price as the very best leather bike saddles, but for people who have to ride often in rainy weather, they will make a bigger improvement in comfort than a good saddle does. If you get a good poncho, take care of it as well as you care for your saddle. Do not wad it up when it's all wet, do not use it as a tarp or compost bin, and be careful as you get on and off the bike with it on, so it doesn't get ripped.

Rain chaps are a relatively new item for rainy-day cyclists. Horsemen have used them for centuries. They protect you from the rain where you need protection, but they don't wad up under your fanny, and you don't get cooked inside them the way you do if you wear full-coverage rain trousers or overalls. Some of the better chaps, available from catalogues like Bike Warehouse (see Addresses) are of the same quality and light material used in making the better rain ponchos. I haven't seen any that are made in different sizes, but these are sure to come. The one-size-fits-all type are OK if you are of normal dimensions.

There are snazzy rubber or gore-tex shoe covers or booties made for wearing over bike-racing shoes, and they even come with a hole in the bottom so your cleats can stick through and fit onto the pedal plate. These covers are very toasty, though. If you live in an area where warm rains are more common than cold ones (like, if you're from Okefenokee, or if you live on the windward side of Mt. Waialeale, in Hawaii) you should simply get a sneaker-type cycling shoe, like the marvelous Bata Biker, and let your feet get wet, then take off the shoes and hang them up to dry at the end of the trip. Wet feet don't seem to be so big a cycling problem as a wet crotch, as long as you don't let your feet *stay* wet for hours on end so weird fungi start growing between your toes. Where the weather is both cold *and* wet, you need a real serious over-the-calf-type booty. Early Winters (see Addresses) has very good ones; they can even be partly opened for ventilation if you heat up inside.

Riding technique can make a huge difference in the rain. First, choose routes with smooth, well-drained pavement and minimal traffic. If you see a puddle of indeterminate depth, look for cars coming up from behind, then swing out and around the puddle when traffic allows. Ride slowly, too, so if you have to go through a puddle or chuckhole, you won't send water spraying, or smash your front wheel into pretzelhood. When going downhill, keep a sharp eye ahead so you can prepare to stop *before* you have to slam on your brakes. To prepare for slowing down, apply your brakes lightly for a moment to whisk all the water off the rims. Then squeeze harder and you'll find that the pads can grip the rim almost as well as they do in dry weather. If you slam on wet brakes, however, they will slip at first, then lock up completely, sending you into a skid, a fall, or worse. Make gentle, leaning turns. You can't lean way over, but you should lean to turn, rather than twitching the handlebars suddenly. Leaning turns will prevent "washout" of your front wheel, and they will also keep the front wheel lined up with the down tube of the bike frame, so less water will splash up and hit you.

When you get to your destination, dry yourself off, of course. But remember to dry your bike off, too. Bounce it up and down a few times so the drops will fly off the wheels, chain, and gears, then run over the frame with a dry rag. It'll take only a moment, and it'll save the metal parts of your bike from rust.

Part II
Alternative Bicycles

Chapter 9
A Three-Speed Station Wagon

THIS IS a workhorse bike. If you'd like to use your bike to tote things around, but you have given up on the idea because your ten-speed just isn't practical, get a three-speed like the one in Illustration 29. If you live in a town or quiet part of a city, you can do more of your commuting and errands on a good old three-speed than you could do on foot, on a ten-speed, or in a car all put together.

Why? Because it's easier and often quicker. You can ride and park where the cars can't. You are sitting up where you can see traffic better than you can on a ten-speed. You can carry more than you can on foot or on a ten-speed. You can use a comfy seat that'll be fine for the short trips. You can use thick tires and tubes to avoid flats. You can even take a kid along. And you can use the bike hard without any worry about getting it scratched and dusty. If it gets to look like a used station wagon, it will be virtually thiefproof. This, in turn, means you don't have to waste time looking for safe parking places, and you don't have to pack a big fancy lock and chain around with you.

The clincher (heh) is that you can toodle along in heavy traffic at almost as good a pace as the fancy bikes, and pass all the backed-up automobiles at every intersection. If you learn some nice shortcuts through back streets and parks, you may even beat some cars to your destination, while having a more pleasant ride as you go. As far as I'm concerned, it's the best possible way to get around. But I'm bound to feel strongly about it; it's my way.

The bike has to be good, though, to make the whole thing work. It can't be one of those fifty-pound tanks we saw when we were kids, the ones they misnamed "middleweights" (middle of *what,* I always wondered). Your workaday three-speed must be built around a light, sturdy frame, and it must have a reliable planet gear hub, like the Sturmy Archer, one that's sturdy and well-known so you can have it repaired at a local shop if it ever needs it.

One bike that fits the description perfectly is the Raleigh Sports, a light three-speed that used to be very common among college students before the days of the ten-speed. Many variations on the basic Raleigh Sports were made by other companies before the ten-speed boom, but these also became rare. The usual three-speed you find in a discount store these days is a heavy thing, made with welded or dip-brazed joints and without lugs. These bikes tend to be unwieldy as well as weaker than the good old Raleigh.

Hunt around to find a good light three-speed with lugs and seamless tubes of high-quality steel like 2130 grade. A new bike with such a frame will cost a bundle, almost as much as an inexpensive ten-speed, but it will last forever, with minimal care. It's hard to find anything, at any price, that lasts. If you can't find a well-made, light three-speed in a retail bike shop, try to find a decent used one. They turn up in garage sales, flea markets, police auctions, and used bike dealers. We got one of our best Raleighs at a rental shop. If you know of a place that rents bikes out near you, go look through their stock of used machines. They may be scratched and flaky, but chances are the shop kept them running well.

You can have fun hand-painting a much-used three-speed. Just take the wheels off, put the chain in a plastic bag, sand the rusty spots, then paint the thing with a brush. You can get wild with your design and color scheme, as long as you don't slosh paint into the bearings or cable housings. You don't want those rolling and sliding parts to get stuck together.

You can make up for a scratched paint job on an old three-speed, but there are several other critical parts that you should check before you buy an old bike. You don't want to buy a lemon that will cost more to fix than it did to purchase.

Spin the wheels. They should go around without lots of gritty grindy noises, and they shouldn't wobble so much they bump against the brake pads on one side and then on the other.

STRONG
CHILD'S SEAT

COMBINATION
LOCK

STURDY
BASKET

DIRT

Illustration **29**   Three-Speed Station Wagon

If the wheel is loose on its bearings or loose in the frame, it can be tightened. It's also OK if just one brake pad is rubbing on one side of the wheel; you can fix that by aligning and adjusting the brake. But if you can see that the rim is bent, so it jumps back and forth between the brakes, or hops up and down (indicating an egg shape of the wheel) then pass up the bike and look for one with wheels that go around nicely.

Pump up the tires if they're soft (they almost always are at garage sales, so take a pump with you when you shop), then take a ride around. Shift the gears to make sure they all work. If a gear is slipping, get off and adjust the indicator chain (see page 108 for hints), then try again. Don't buy a three-speed with only two speeds. If one is ruined, the others may go soon, and rebuilding a three-speed hub is expensive and time consuming.

Get a bike with a frame that's about the right size for you, so you can raise or lower the seat to such a position that when you sit on it your leg straightens at the bottom of each pedal stroke. Make especially sure the frame isn't too big if it's a men's style and you plan to put a child seat on the back of the bike. You have to hoist your leg over the bar to get on and off; if you try to swing your leg over the back of the bike cowboy-style, you'll tend to knock the block off any kid who happens to be sitting there.

Finally, see if the bike will coast straight ahead on a flat surface if you take your hands off the handlebars. Even if you aren't good at riding no-handed, you can get the thing coasting straight, take your hands off the grips for just a second, and see if the bike wants to track straight or veer off to the same side every time. If it veers, the frame or forks must be bent. You'll waste energy riding that catty-whompus thing around. If you can't get a clear idea of the frame's straightness from your hands-off riding, have someone stand right behind you as you ride directly away from him or her; this is easiest to do if you coast down a gentle slope. If the friend can see both of your wheels where they touch the ground (in other words, if the back wheel isn't following exactly behind the front one), the bike has a bent frame.

Illustration 30
Frame Cockeyed

Why worry so much about a bent frame? Glad you asked. It makes the difference between fighting the bike and flowing along on it. A bent frame makes the bike hard to balance and steer with heavy loads aboard. There are probably thousands of ex-cyclists who gave up riding because they thought they couldn't balance well enough, when in fact the problem was that the bike was always trying to go two directions at once. Straightening a bent frame is a job for a real pro, and even the pros can't manage it in some cases, so avoid any second-hand three-speed that is out of line.

If a prospective bike covers the three essentials (the wheels go around, the gears work, and the frame is straight), don't worry too much about small problems with other parts. Leaky tires can be patched or replaced. Frayed saddles can be fixed with duct tape or replaced with nice, comfy new saddles like the ones shown in Illustrations 26 and 31. Bent handlebars, rusty brake cables, and broken fenders can all be fixed for a few bucks and a couple of hours of work. To help you get this stuff together, read through the following paragraphs and fix or replace whatever you need to get the bike in good working order.

Start with the seat and handlebars; get ones that suit your size and physique, and adjust them so you can ride comfortably, even if the bike is heavily loaded and you are threading your way through heavy traffic.

The handlebars may be wide or narrow, and the ends may point straight out, or almost straight back. By twisting the bar in the stem that holds it (loosen the binder bolt in the stem so the bars move freely), you can make the ends point down, level, or up. To me, the best combination is a pair of bars that are a little wider than my shoulders, with the ends pointing back a bit, and also pointing down just a few degrees. The handlebars in Illustration 29 are set this way. You may like the racier little French bars that point almost straight out, so you lean forward when you're riding. This position is good for longer rides; it lowers your wind resistance when you bend forward like that. The position is not so nice in slow traffic riding; it makes it harder to stop and start, and harder to turn your head to check out cars coming up from behind. The racer's dropped or "maes" curved bars can be put on a three-speed, but they are even harder to use in traffic.

Whichever bars you settle on, make sure they have good solid grips on the ends. If the bike has old grips that have worn away so the sharp metal end of the bar pokes through the plastic, replace the grips for sure. If it's hard to get the old grips off, take the bike to the shop where you buy your new grips. They can blast your old grips off by putting an air hose in one end and plugging the hole in the grip on the other side with their thumb. Clean the bars off and put a dab of soapy water on the new grips so it'll be easy to get them on by yourself. Twist them on, pushing the end as you turn the grip. Don't use a hammer on the end of the thing; you'll just perforate it so it's as dangerous as the worn-out grip you took off.

The seat or saddle on a three-speed station wagon bike should be strong, form-fitting, and comfortable over a long haul. This may not be the seat that has the most padding. Over-cushy

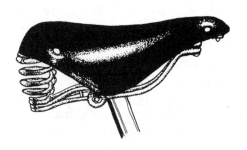

Illustration **31**

Classic Sit-down Bike Seat

ones look weird and chafe you too much. Most of you will prefer a leather or leather-covered plastic saddle with a narrow front end and a wide-flared back end to fit the wider part of *your* back end. If you ride in an area where there are bumpy streets, or a city where they pave the middle of the street nicely but leave the shoulder a maze of patches, dips, cracks, and gratings (this is the way most cities do things), you should find a seat with strong springs under the back part. They don't have to be full-on coiled springs like those in Illustration 31. If the wires that hold up the rear edge of the saddle make a loop, this will be adequate in most cases. If you are unusually light or heavy, you may have trouble finding a seat with suspension that works for you. In this case look into the anatomical plastic, foam, and leather seats such as those discussed on page 74. If you get a good leather seat, especially one that has been pre-treated so it will break in more quickly, make sure it has a nut under the front end that can be tightened to take up any slack that may develop as the seat ages and stretches. On some seats this nut is almost impossible to reach with a wrench. If yours is that way, you can often cut a slot in the end of the bolt with a hacksaw, then use a wrench to hold the nut still while you tighten the bolt with a screwdriver.

Get your seat mounted properly, with the solid band that clamps around the seat post facing toward the FRONT of the bike. Leave the binder bolt in that clamp loose until you have adjusted the seat so it is pointing straight forward (line up the front of the seat with the center of the top tube that's below it) and tipped the way you like it. I like the front end of the seat tipped up about five degrees or so, but others like the seat level, and some even prefer to have the seat tipped down a bit. The only problem with having the seat tilted forward is that you always have the feeling your weight is being pitched onto the handlebars. Your arms have to work much more. If you try to sit farther back on the seat to prevent sore arms, your duff hangs over the rear edge of the seat and the rim of it digs into you. Ouch.

If you set a good seat on the level or with the front up a bit, on the other hand, you'll get this great, balanced, cushioned. chafeless ride. Ahhhh. One can't get very excited about bike seats without sounding like a bad stand-up (or is it sit-down?) comedian, but without getting tacky I can say that after years of riding on a good bicycle seat, you just feel nice and comfy, the minute you're in the saddle, and you stay comfy all the time, whether you're riding up to the corner for some milk and bread, or taking a long pleasure jaunt with your kid and a picnic lunch aboard. I'm sure seasoned old cowboys must feel the same way about their saddles, and no stand-up comics kid them about where *they* sit down. A good bike seat deserves more respect!

Make sure your comfy seat isn't too high or low, either. It should be at that height where your leg extends fully when each pedal reaches the bottom of its stroke. Not so high that you have to reach tippy-toe down there, but no so low that your knees fold up and hit your adam's apple at the top of each pedal stroke.

The other basics for a good three-speed include sturdy fenders, reflectors for the pedals and for both the front and back of the bike, and a simple, reliable lock.

Fenders usually come with the bike, but they are often bent, cracked, and loose, and the braces are always bent in or out. All you usually have to do is straighten the braces (you can do it by hand, and when they are straight, the fender will be lined up so it doesn't hit the tire) and tighten all the bolts and nuts that hold the thing to the bike. If the bolts are rusty, replace them.

Look at the reflectors on the pedals, on the rear fender, and on the front of the bike. If any are broken or missing, replace them and bolt the new ones on firmly. If the pedal reflectors are wrecked, you have to replace the pedals. You can do this yourself if you have a narrow-profile wrench that fits the flat sides of the pedal spindle, right next to where it screws

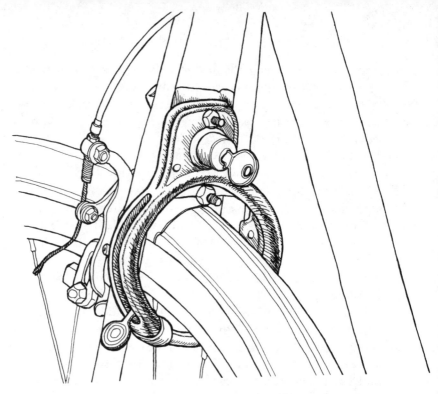

Illustration **32** A   The People's Bike Lock

into the crank. Just make sure you screw and unscrew the left
pedal BACKWARD (it unscrews clockwise, and screws in counter-
clockwise). It's nice to have a little generator light on the front
wheel of your three-speed, or even a light with batteries, but
these things always seem to get beat up, or left on, so they
don't work when you really need them. A better idea is to have
a leg light or two, like the ones in Illustration 10, and maybe a
little clip on the handlebar that you can put a flashlight or a
"Wonder" light into.

Get a simple combination or key lock for your bike. I have
a really convenient one that a friend brought me from China.
It's a lock for places where the threat of theft isn't too great.
They use them all over the People's Republic and in some of the
more civilized parts of Europe. I'm proud to say that this little
town is also safe enough (or is it that my bike is funky enough?)
to use the Chinese lock. It is very basic. It's attached to the bike
frame by the rear brake, and when you push a button, a little
bar slides between the spokes and locks the wheel so the bike

can't roll. When you turn the key in the lock, the bar slides back into it, and you ride away. No fuss, no muss, no chains and cables to get tangled in the works. You can use a long-hasp bike lock in the same place, but you have to hang the thing somewhere else on the bike (like under the seat on the seat rails) while it isn't in use. If there are modern bike parking stands where you live, the kind that have a cable attached for each bike, you can thread the cable through your frame or front wheel and lock it to the rear wheel with your simple long-hasp bike lock.

If you have to lock the bike in various theft-prone places, the best locking option is a small padlock and a short chain that's covered with either vinyl or a piece of old inner tube, so it won't scratch up the bike too much. If you get a chain that's just the right length, you can lock it around your waist while you are riding, as the bikers do in much of Europe. It's handy there, and it won't fall off or get stuck in the works, as it often does if you keep it coiled up in the basket or wrapped around the bike frame under your seat. A short section of vinyl-covered cable may be used in the same way, but it won't be so easy to handle.

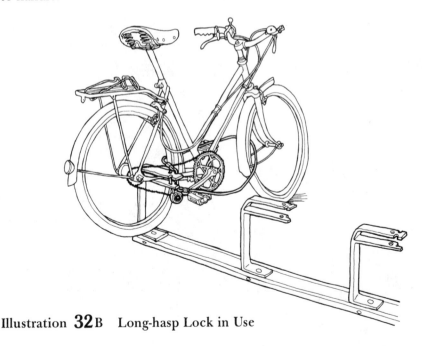

Illustration **32**B   Long-hasp Lock in Use

The only trouble with carrying the lock and chain around your middle is that you may draw snide remarks about it. People say it looks like a chastity belt, or like some kind of new S&M outfit. Such commentary says more about the speaker than it does about the subject. It should slide off you like water off a duck. If it persists to the point that it really offends you, all you have to do is unlock the nasty thing and whirl it around your head a few times with a sort of a nonchalant Marlon Brando grin on your face. This will tend to silence critics and snickerers, although it hardly becomes a peaceful cyclist.

A Pack-Horse Basket

Spend a little extra bread to put a solid, convenient basket on your three-speed station wagon. Don't leave a rusty old shoebox-size one on the bike, if that's what came on it. If it has one of

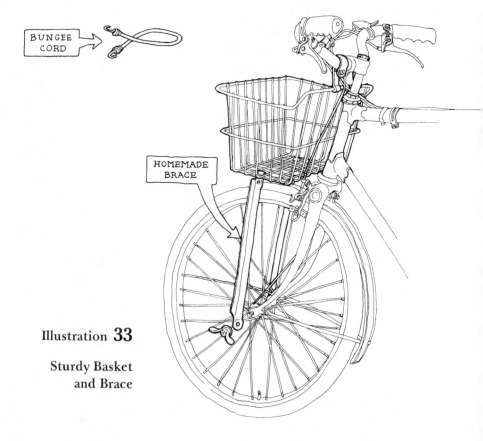

BUNGEE CORD

HOMEMADE BRACE

Illustration **33**

Sturdy Basket and Brace

those phony plastic Easter baskets strapped to the handlebars, tear the thing off and throw it as far out of your life as you can. I mean, do you want a toy, or do you want to bring home the groceries on your bike?

You need a basket that's big enough and strong enough to hold at least two full shopping bags. Or a 25-pound sack of fertilizer for the garden, or a volleyball and net, or any of a thousand other loads. Obviously, the bigger it is, the less often you have to forsake the bike and use a gas-gulping car to go pick something up downtown. We have two station wagon bikes in the family. One has a basket that measures a generous foot-and-a-half wide by a foot front-to-back by 6 inches deep. The other one has a basket that is smaller (14 by 9 inches) but deeper (8 inches). You can put two full shopping bags in the big basket, but if you have a taller, tippy single bag, it is more secure in the smaller, deeper basket. Both baskets are made of welded wire, and both have heavy-duty wires or straps running under them from front to back and around the sides, so the load is distributed between the braces and the handlebar straps. Avoid baskets that are made entirely of light wire; they'll bend and break if you don't balance the load in them perfectly.

The braces that come with most baskets are chintzy. There was a time when they made them strong enough to hold up anything that would fit in the basket. Those old pre-chintzy days were great for basket braces, but there were other problems back then, like the fact that most bikes weighed a ton! The modern braces are especially weak if you have a tall bike and you attach each basket brace with the axle through the lowest hole in that row down at the bottom of the brace.

The holes in the braces that are above the axle make the brace really weak. Some day, when you lean your bike on a low wall, or allow it to fall over on a curb or something, the weak brace will bend at one of the holes. You may straighten it, but it'll bend again at the same place the next time you put a heavy load in the basket. You'll probably go on bending it a little and straightening it a little until one day, when you have a huge load of tomatoes, soft plums, and jars of jam stuffed into the basket, the brace will break, the broken end will get caught in your front wheel, and you and your produce will proceed to spread yourselves down the road in a wide splatter.

Illustration **34**

To avoid this scenario, replace the chintzy braces with homemade superbraces. Take the stock ones off first. If they are riveted at the top ends, use a drill or metal file to cut away the dented end of each rivet, then pull out the rivet to remove the brace. Measure the length of a brace and go to a good hardware store or building supply to buy a length of 1-inch angle aluminum (like angle iron, but much lighter) that's long enough to make two braces. Hang the basket on your bike so the support straps go straight down from the handlebars, as in Illustration 33, then measure the length the braces need to be. If the stock braces were the right length, you can use one for a template to measure and mark the new braces for cutting and drilling. Make sure you get the new braces exactly the right length, so that when you hook them up, the handlebar straps will hang straight down and the bottom of the basket will be level. If things don't come out that way, the basket will be weak and wobbly when heavily loaded. Cut the angle aluminum to length and drill the holes for the axle and the small bolt that will attach the upper end to the small clip on the bottom of the basket. It's a nice idea to make the lower cut diagonal, as shown. This facilitates tightening and loosening your axle bolts, and takes off a sharp corner that would tend to stick out and catch on things or cut the shins of innocent passersby. Match the braces by setting them together to make sure the lengths are equal and the holes are drilled in the same place. If you don't have a drill that's big enough to make that large hole for the axle, take the braces to a good bike shop; they'll have the drill, and they'll probably cut the hole for free if you bought the basket from them in the first place.

When you get your sturdy basket mounted correctly (make sure the brake and gear cables are free and untangled, as shown in Illustration 33), tighten all the nuts firmly, and you'll be ready to carry all kinds of loads on your local errands. If the bolts that tighten the handlebar straps are so long they stick back menacingly where your knees may scrape them when you stand up on the pedals to ride up a steep hill, saw the bolt ends off and file the cut smooth with a metal file.

Two handy gadgets to use with your basket, items you should carry in it at all times, are a bungee cord and a little cloth backpack. The cord can hold down tall or flappy loads, and the pack is great for delicate items or anything that's left over when you have filled the basket.

A Sturdy Child Seat

If you have young children, you don't have to truck them around in a two-ton car, any more than you have to use the two-ton gas hog to run up to the store for groceries. If your child weighs less than 60 pounds, and you don't have to take the kid more than a couple of miles, why not use a bike? Even if you have two kids, one an infant and one in the 2-5-year range, you can take the big one in the child seat and the little one in a pack (such as the Gerry pack) on your back. This is impossible on a ten-speed with racing handlebars, but on a nice sit-up three-speed like the one in Illustration 29 it will work fine. When the kids get bigger, you can carry them in a trailer (see page 113), or, even better, teach the older one to ride along with you (see page 126).

There are two basic types of children's seats. The first is the classic squared-off strap steel frame with a couple of flat cushions, as shown in Illustration 35. A standard-setting brand of this type is Troxel. They make seats widely marketed by Schwinn and mail-order catalogues. I have found the basic Troxel/Schwinn-type seat to be safe, sturdy, and practical over years of use. There are similar strap-steel seats made of thinner, weaker metal, with flimsy little bolts and nuts holding the joints together. These work OK if you have a lightweight kid, and they are lighter themselves, so they are attractive if you're trying to keep the weight of your bike down, but you have to watch these light seats like a hawk. They can come loose or start waggling around until the metal straps break or come apart at the joints, and if this happens, the child can easily get a foot stuck in the spokes, or, what's worse, fall directly backward to the pavement. I've seen the results of both types of accident, and I strongly recommend you get one of the heavier but safer Troxel/Schwinn child seats, or one that is as sturdy and well-designed.

There is another whole group of child seats, made with light tubular steel frames and molded plastic chassis that surround the child and keep its feet out of the wheel completely. The idea of shielding the child this way is a good one, and on some models, such as the Firestone convertible and the Schwinn/Troxel High-back, the frame is sturdy and the whole unit works well. But on many seats of this molded plastic type, the manufacturers tried to keep the weight down by using thin, weak tubing for the frame. The tubing is mashed flat at the ends where it attaches to the bike frame, and is even weaker at these points. After you use the seat for a while, it begins to wag back and forth, the metal begins to fatigue, which makes it wag more and more, until the metal breaks at the critical juncture of the bike and the seat. When the seat breaks loose it may sag slowly over to one side, or it may snap completely free at the top and fall straight backward, so your child's head cracks down on the pavement.

Clearly, you want to avoid weak-framed child seats of any description. If you already have a seat that you feel may be questionable, get a good helmet for your child (Pro-tec now makes helmets for small heads), and check the seat frame often at the point where it attaches to the bike frame just under your

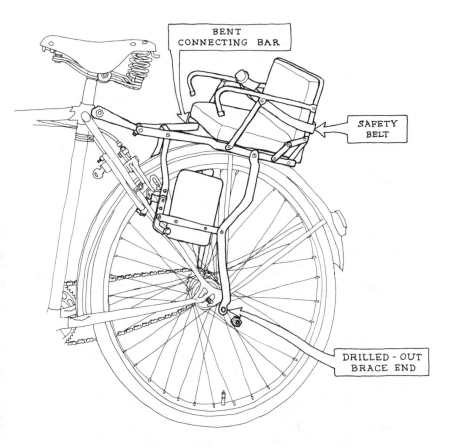

BENT CONNECTING BAR

SAFETY BELT

DRILLED-OUT BRACE END

Illustration **35**   Mounting Child Seat

seat. If the child seat can wag back and forth, and tightening the mounting bolts doesn't make it any more rigid, assume that the weak metal of the frame is fatiguing; take the child seat off your bike, NOW, and replace it with one of the stronger models.

The stronger seats have frames that are noticeably sturdier. They are easy to pick out at a store. They are more expensive when new, but they're so sturdy you can buy a secondhand one without any fear, as long as it hasn't been abused. We find them for friends at flea markets, garage sales, and rummage sales, and they usually cost about a third what they do in a shop.

To mount a child seat like the Troxel type, you may have to do some custom fitting, unless your bike is a Schwinn. This seems like a big pain, but it's well worth the trouble to gain peace of mind when your kid is riding along back there.

The first parts of the child seat you attach to the bike are the lower ends of the braces. That way the seat will stay more or less in place while you do the trickier attachment under the bike seat. On many three-speeds there are sturdy mounting bolts holding the fender braces. Undo these, take off the washers if there are any, and put the bolt through the fender brace, through the child seat brace, and then through the hole in the lug of the bike frame. If the hole is threaded, so much the better; screw the bolt in until it's tight, then tighten the nut on for double safety. For triple safety, you can get black high-carbon steel bolts for the braces; they are extra-strong, so they'll *never* break.

If your bike doesn't have any fender brace bolts, or if the bolts are dinky little things that look much too weak to hold up a 40-to-50-pound kid securely, you can drill a big hole in the end of your child seat brace and put it onto the rear axle of the bike. To do this you need a 7/16-inch high-speed drill bit that's good and sharp. It may be a job you have to take to a shop to make sure the holes are the right size and drilled in such a way they don't weaken the end of the brace.

Once the holes are drilled, loosen the little sleeve and take it off the end of the indicator. At this point, if you have a Sturmey/Archer-type hub, you have to unscrew the whole indicator chain before you can unscrew and remove the big axle nut. On Shimano hubs, you unscrew the big nut and the chain comes with it. When you get those parts off either type of hub, treat them with care and keep them in a clean, safe place so they don't get lost or dirty.

Take the big nut off the other end of the rear axle, and if there are washers under the nuts, take them off too. The end of the brace will act as a washer from now on. Slide the braces over the ends of the axles after you have drilled out the holes in them to 7/16-inch, then spin the axle nuts on by hand. At this point you need help to hold the wheel straight, with the chain tight, and the child seat sticking up where you want it. Get a friend or your kid to hold the wheel so it is centered between the stays and back far enough to keep the chain in its almost-tight adjustment. You can hold the seat up so it is level as you tighten the nuts down with a wrench. Don't tighten them all the way yet (you may have to move the child seat a bit to get it lined up under the bike's seat) but get them tight enough to keep everything from flobbing around. If you have a Sturmey/ Archer hub, make sure the indicator chain is clean, then turn it back into the axle. Don't turn it in hard; just twist it in gently with your fingers until it reaches the end of the threads, then back it off about a quarter turn, so it can flex around and connect to the end of the cable. Turn the sleeve onto the threaded end of the indicator, no matter which make of hub you have, and adjust the thing so when it is in the middle gear (labeled 2 or N on the gear lever) you can just see the shoulder at the end of the smooth shaft sticking out beyond the end of the axle, as in Illustration 37A. On some Shimano gear hubs, there is a different sort of axle nut, one with an arrow that points at a line or at an N when the thing is adjusted correctly to the middle gear. When you have your indicator and cable adjusted right, whichever kind you have, tighten the locknut on the threaded end of the indicator against the sleeve that's attached to the cable, so the thing won't go out of adjustment on you.

Now you have to fuss around with the joints at the front of the child seat so it will be level and as far forward as possible when you attach it to the binder bolt under the bike's seat. To get mine right, I had to angle the connecting bars down, as shown in Illustration 35, and bend the front of the seat frame up a little so the seat would come out level. Do any such bending with care so you don't weaken the metal. If you have to bend a tubular framepiece, find a length of pipe to slip over the tube and bend it a slight bit at a time, moving the pipe after each bending effort, so you don't crimp the tube and weaken it. Get the seat level and as far forward as it will go, but make sure it isn't so far forward and down that your heels hit the stirrups for your kid's feet.

When the seat is adjusted the way you want it, undo the binder bolt for the bike's seat post, then take it out and push it through the holes in the end of the connecting bar as well as the holes in the bike frame. If the holes in the connecting bar are too small, widen them out with a drill or a reamer. If the binder bolt is not long enough to make it all the way through, get a longer one. Don't use just any old stove bolt, though, get a real binder bolt that's made of strong, high-grade steel, so it won't strip out or bend. That binder bolt has to be quite strong just to hold the seat post. Putting the child seat on it adds another big and important burden. If the binder bolt has a little metal bump under the head that's supposed to fit in a slot (it's called a "dog" by mechanics), file a nick into the hole through the connecting bar so the dog can fit into it and hold the bolt still while you tighten the nut. Use a box-end or socket wrench to do the tightening, and make sure it fits the nut exactly, so you can get that bolt as tight as possible without stripping the threads.

There are few child seats that attach to the seat stays rather than the binder bolt. Make sure the clamps for this type fit your stays tightly, and get the bolts extra-tight, so they won't come loose. You may even want to use a thread adhesive such as Loctite to make sure those critical bolts stay tight. If you live near a large, well-stocked hardware and industrial supply store, you can get aircraft nuts, the kind with a nylon ring inserted in them. Tighten these supernuts on well and you won't have to fear for the safety of your child passengers.

If there is only a single bolt that tightens the clamps on both stays, you should really replace it with two bolts. Drill holes for them in the two clamp plates and use a rack support, such as the one shown on page 59, to make sure the child seat won't slip around, even if it does get a little loose.

On many child seats, the cushion is loose; it will rattle and flap around unless you get a bungee cord and strap it down tight. This extra bungee can come in handy for special loading situations, I've found. I remember carrying two 8-foot 2 X 4 boards home on the bike once. I attached them with two bungee cords so they ran horizontally from the side of the kid seat to the side of the basket, much the way pipe is carried along the fenders of a plumber's truck. The only catch was that I had to keep the front bungee cord loose so I could steer. It looked weird, but it worked like a charm.

Tips on Using the Three-Speed

If you have built up a solid workhorse bike like the one in Illustration 29, you will soon find that it is capable of carrying more than is convenient. For instance, if you put a gallon of apple juice and a gallon or so of milk and some groceries in the basket, and a 35-pound squirming rascal in the child seat, the bike will be hard to hold upright, much less to mount without kicking the kid in the head or getting your leg hung up on the top tube. And once you get on the bike, it's hard to get moving on it. If you do any slow maneuvering at all, the loaded bike will handle like a drunk hippo. And if you manage to get your gurgling and squirmy load home, you may have trouble finding a place to lean the bike or even a flat place to set it on its kickstand. And if you get it balanced, all the kid has to do is lean over to one side or kick and fuss a bit while being lifted out of the seat, and the bike will topple, sending apple juice crashing to the ground, where it will mingle happily with the milk and dirt, defying any efforts to clean it up.

Loading and unloading the bike takes a little finesse. The process can be made much easier if you install a neat new gadget called a Flickstand. This piece of Yankee ingenuity is

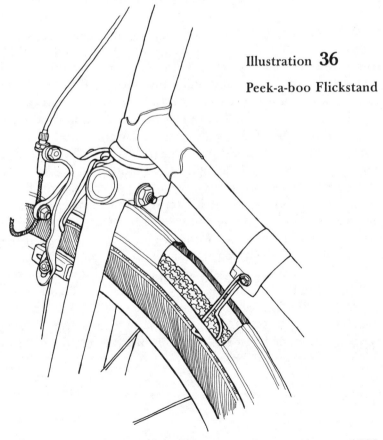

Illustration **36**

Peek-a-boo Flickstand

nothing more than a little curved wire that clamps to your bike's down tube. When you fold it down, it blocks the front wheel so it can't roll or steer. To mount the Flickstand on a three-speed, first check to make sure it is long enough (you must use the longer of the two wires included with the kit) to reach from the bike frame to the tire. If it is, use a hacksaw to cut out a square section of the fender at the point where the down tube comes closest to the tire. Then put the plastic strap around the tube, install the wire and cinch up the Flickstand by tightening the little bolt and nut (see Illustration 36). If you have trouble installing the Flickstand correctly, see page 68 for further instructions. When your front wheel is held still by the Flickstand, you can lean the bike against almost anything and it'll stay put, as long as you don't tilt it way over or set it on such a steep slope that it rolls when you put your load on the bike. When you're all loaded and balanced on the bike, just reach down and flick the wire loop up and you're set to go. The Flickstand is available from some bike shops and the better catalogues (see Addresses).

For bikes that have too much space between the front wheel and the frame for a Flickstand, you can use a thick rubber band to do the same thing the Flickstand does. All you have to do is turn the wheel until the tire valve is up near the down tube, then hook one end of the band around the valve, wrap the band around the down tube, and slip the other end over the valve, too, as shown in Illustration 25B. This process is hard to do if you are holding a squirmy kid or an awkward bag of groceries. It will work if you can get used to it, though, and for those who have lots of space between the frame and tire, it's the answer. You can hook the rubber band around the brake handle post while you aren't using it; it's easy to get out of that storage place, even with one hand. And if you find a convenient wall to lean the bike against, you can hold the kid or groceries with one hand, apply the rubber band stand with the other, and go off with the knowledge that the bike won't roll or steer and tip over. The bike stands still while you're loading it, too. When everything's loaded you can use both hands to get the band off the wheel and onto the brake post.

There are other tricks that make it easier to load and mount your three-speed station wagon. If you need to carry a load and a child, put the load on the bike first, and don't lift the little wriggler into the seat until both your hands are free to contain the kid and balance the bike. Don't try to balance a loaded bike without a wall or pole to lean it against, even if you have a good Flickstand. If your load is made up of some sturdy items, like cans of juice or sacks of potatoes, put these in the basket first. Put perishables like loaves of bread or little boxes of strawberries on top of the basket load, or in a little cloth backpack. If there's too much for both your backpack and the basket, give some dropable items, like a can of tomato paste, to your back-seat driver. Children of certain ages can't be relied upon to carry certain things, of course, but most kids of most ages above two will enjoy the chance to help out. If you have flat items, like notebooks, magazines, or picture books, you can strap them onto the flat back of the child seat with a bungee cord, or they can go on the seat, under the kid. The bungee can be used to hold the seat pads in place when they aren't holding flat loads down.

When the bike is nicely loaded and you have flicked the Flickstand up or undone the rubber band, you have to meet the challenge of getting ON the thing without knocking the kid's head off or catching your cuff on the bike's top tube and tipping it over.

If you have a women's model bike, or a mixte-frame bike with the top tube or tubes down low, you can step on and off the bike easily. It's harder to get off a men's bike, with the top tube set up high. If you have a background of gymnastics or ballet, you can do a very high kick and swing your leg all the way over the head of your child passenger. Otherwise, you have to fold your leg and stick your foot over the top tube. I've found it easiest to do this if the bike is sitting on flat ground or even down in the street lower than where I'm standing on the curb.

If you hold the handlebar that's nearest to you with one hand, and hold the seat with the other, you can tip the bike slightly toward you as you lift your foot over the top tube. I've found that it helps to tap the top tube with your toe as you lift your foot over. This tap steadies the bike at that awkward moment, and gives your foot a bit more lift to get all the way over the top tube without getting snagged. It looks a little odd (I bet even Fred Astaire never did a top hat routine on a top

tube!) but it does help you balance at the moment when you
really need help. Of course, all cable clips should be kept away
from the middle of the top tube, to keep your cuff-snagging to
an absolute minimum. Once your leg is over the top tube, get it
back down to the ground in a hurry and grab both handlebars
before the bike starts to tip, steer, and yaw out of control.

Start riding quickly, so you don't weave and wobble
around precariously before you can pick up speed. Keep this in
mind at every intersection, too. Slow to a stop smoothly but
quickly, and take off briskly, so you can get up to an easy-
balancing speed in no time. Most problems people have with the
three-speed station wagon occur when the bike is standing still
or moving very slowly. All the weight and bulk you carry on
such a bike travels more smoothly at speed. If you get the bike
going fast enough to cruise comfortably in middle gear, this will
make for less erratic weaving and wobbling around, and thus
make riding less work for you. Middle gear is the most efficient
one, anyway. The other two are not direct drive, so some of
your work gets soaked up by the spinning cogs in the gear hub.

Gear Adjustment

It is critical to have all three speeds on your station wagon bike,
even though you'll use the middle one most of the time. On
up- and downhill roads, the high and low gears make a huge
difference. Learn how to adjust your own gears on your trusty
three-speed, so you'll never strip them or lose one when you
really need it.

Illustration **37**A

Sturmey Archer
Three-Speed Adjustment

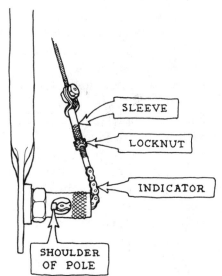

SLEEVE

LOCKNUT

INDICATOR

SHOULDER
OF POLE

Set the gear lever in the middle gear (it will say N or 2), then crouch down by the right side of the rear hub and look where the indicator goes inside the axle. You should see something like the Sturmey/Archer or Shimano units shown in Illustration 37. On the Sturmey/Archer, look into the round hole in the axle nut; the shoulder at the end of the smooth pole that goes into the axle should just show beyond the end of the axle. On the Shimano, the metal arrow should point directly at the line in the middle of the peephole. If you have taken off washers that were around the axle and put on a child seat with the brace around the axle, you may have changed things a bit so it's hard to get an exact reading of the indicator adjustment, but the adjustment should still be the same.

To change the setting if its wrong, loosen the sleeve and locknut at the cable end of the indicator, reset the sleeve either tighter (clockwise) or looser (counter-clockwise), then lock the locknut against the sleeve again with your fingers. Turn the pedals forward with your hands. They should meet resistance immediately, indicating that the middle gear is engaged.

Move the gear control lever into the lowest gear position (marked L or 1) and try the pedals again. If the lever is hard to pull into the low position, backpedal a bit to let things mesh in the gear hub. If it's still impossible to get the bike into low gear, the cable must be too tight. Loosen the sleeve and locknut on the indicator and turn the sleeve one or two turns counter-clockwise before tightening up the locknut. It should now be possible to move the gear lever into the lowest position, and the

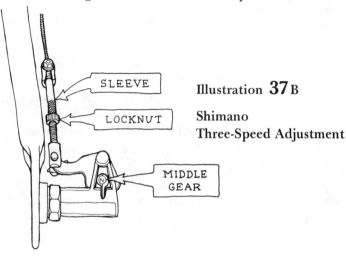

Illustration **37** B

Shimano
Three-Speed Adjustment

cable should be tight, so the indicator is pulled all the way out (or pushed all the way in, if it's a Shimano). Try turning the pedals forward by hand. They should meet resistance right away, indicating that the gears are engaged.

To test the high gear, move the lever to H or 3. The cable should now have a little slack in it, and once again, the pedals should meet resistance if you turn them forward. If you get positive results in all three gears, hop on the bike and ride it around, shifting the gears for hills, stops, and starts. Make extra-sure you can shift into and out of the middle gear without slippage. The most common mistake is to have the indicator a little loose, so that when you shift from the lowest to the middle gear, the little clutch gizmo in the hub goes a little too far, and the gears don't fully mesh, but rather grind and gnash, wearing all their edges into round and useless nubs.

If the gears don't pass your test, check the adjustment again, then check the cable and lever to make sure they aren't jammed, rusted, or ruined in some way. Replace them if they are shot, then adjust the gears as above.

It's comforting to know you have a good gear set-up, and one that's adjusted properly. It means you won't have those painful and embarassing falls onto your top tube, caused by gear slippage. It also means that your gears will last much longer than they would if they were allowed to go sloppy to the point of stripping and gnashing. If you have a bike that has been so abused in the past that the gears tend to slip and strip no matter how well they are adjusted, there is no alternative to getting the parts or the whole wheel replaced. If the wheel is straight and there is a mechanic in your area who is a known ace at rebuilding three-speeds, you can have the thing rebuilt, but in most places, the safest idea is to get a whole new wheel. If you are in doubt about whether your local mechanic is a three-speed hub ace, just find out if the mechanic in question loves playing around with Chinese puzzles. If he or she does, the chances are good that your three-speed will be fixed carefully and correctly. Any mechanic who is not a puzzle fan probably won't have the patience to do a good job on your gear hub, even if he or she has learned how to do it at a Schwinn or Raleigh training school. I love both hubs and puzzles, but then I'm a tinkering fool, and if most mechanics lavished the kind of time and effort on a hub that I do, they'd all go broke and/or blind. Very few normal people share my delight for slippery pawl springs, thrust rings, and axle keys. So if you feel that your local mechanic is too sane or too profit-oriented to do justice to your hub, go ahead and spend a small pile of cash to get a new wheel. Then promise yourself to check the adjustment of the indicator now and then, keeping the hub in good adjustment so it will last the life of the bike.

Other Maintenance

The three-speed station wagon bike needs very little care other than keeping the gears adjusted. Keep a light oil on the chain, enough that it looks a little moist, but not so much that drips of oil fly off and hit your legs. Keep the tires inflated enough so that even when the bike is loaded down, you don't hit the rim of the rear wheel when you go over a bump (for tips on airing tires, see page 4). Make sure the brakes are adjusted so they are fully applied when you have squeezed the handle only halfway to the handlebar. And check the nuts and bolts that hold the child seat together.

That's all there is to it. You don't even have to keep the bike superclean, as long as you keep it out of the rain and fog. In fact, a little dust and dirt on an old three-speed act like theft insurance. There are very, very few thieves who have a taste for dusty old black three-speed bikes with baskets and child seats on them. For one thing, most thieves are after status items they can show off on, then sell to a fence for a good price. Dusty three-speeds are zero on the status scale, and almost worthless on the resale market. They are much too utilitarian. I like the idea that part of the reason my three-speed has never been stolen is precisely because it looks so useful. Maybe I'm a romantic fool, but I also think that even thieves can see that it's bad Karma to steal a bike someone obviously depends on so much. It would be like stealing a farmer's favorite old tractor.

So don't dust and polish your trusty station wagon bike. Let it get seasoned and old-looking. Do take care of its vital needs, though, just as you would take care of the needs of any often-used, much-loved tool.

Chapter 10
The Bicycle Truck

IF YOU want to carry more than a few groceries and one small kid, you'll need more than a three-speed station wagon bike. You'll need a two-, three-, or four-wheel pedal truck. The idea of using a bike as a truck may come as a shock to you. It seems downright un-American. It was probably investigated by the House Subcommittee during the paranoid fifties. If it wasn't looked into, it should have been. I mean, the Chinese have been using those flat-bed trikes ever since Mao took the reins. And everybody knows how the North Vietnamese carried all those supplies down the Ho Chi Minh Trail. . . .

If we really looked into the uses of the bicycle around the world, we'd find that America is one of the few places where the bike truck *hasn't* been used effectively. Even in the capital of our closest neighbor to the south, bicycle trucks have been used for a great deal of inner city transport. Lately, however, as Mexico has begun to produce more and more oil, there have been fewer and fewer pedal trucks on the streets of Mexico City.

The reason is simple. If you've got cheap oil, why should you push the pedals? Pedaling a truck is hard work, even on perfectly flat terrain. On hills it is impossible. You have to get off and push. And this, this pushing and sweating up hills, this is *absolutely* un-American. Alas, the equation that explains the declining use of bike trucks in Mexico can also be reversed; as less and less gas is sold at higher and higher prices in the U.S., and other modern countries, the pedal-powered truck will make more and more sense.

This may lead to a new form of development: a so-called "developed" country borrowing technology from the under-developed ones. We might even have to call on a Chinese or Mexican version of the Peace Corps to convert our lazy, gas-pedal dependence into the kind of vigorous self-determination that is required for the use of a bicycle truck. Can you imagine a dignified foreign emissary of the "Small is Beautiful" philosophy, pedaling up to a truck stop somewhere along Interstate 80, stepping off a trusty flat-bed, and trying to talk the coffee-shop crowd of teamsters into turning in their rigs for ones like

Illustration **38** Dan and Fergie's Truck.

hers? It sounds like a mad nightmare. But certainly no more crazy than some of the things *our* emissaries have been trying to talk the other peoples of the world into.

In fact, I think more Americans will pick up the bicycle truck idea in the next few years than "underdeveloped" people will pick up our high-tech ideas. After all, it is both patriotic and self-reliant to ride a bike and avoid using OPEC oil, and both self-reliance and patriotism are strong American traits. Besides, Yankee ingenuity has already brought forth a very good, light bicycle-truck, a trailer that can be added onto the backs of most bikes and used to carry anything from a couple of kids to a heavy load of lumber.

The Bugger is a light two-wheeled trailer, designed for use on ten-speeds, but just as practical if used behind a sit-up-style bike. There are also heavier and cheaper bike trailers that can be used for small local loads, and even some custom superlight trailers made for high performance.

All of the American trailers are a little harder to handle in close quarters than the traditional pedal trucks, and they are hard to back into and out of parking spaces. But they have the attraction of being detachable, so you don't have to lug the extra weight and size of the vehicle around with you on your commuting and pleasure rides.

You can also get a three-wheeled cycle with a large basket mounted between the two rear wheels. There's a good selection of trike trucks with two front wheels for industrial uses as well (see Addresses). But these trikes are for carrying heavy loads on very flat areas, or for riders who do not have good balance and quick reflexes. Trikes are usually too heavy to take up and down hills, and they are dangerous if you ride on surfaces that

Illustration **39**   People's Truck

slope sideways, or if you ride around corners fast. They tip over without warning. For instance, if you are riding along a nice level sidewalk, and come to a sloped driveway that causes the sidewalk to dip and slant out toward the street, you can flip onto your ear before you know what's happening. So if you want to spend a bundle of dough to get a more utilitarian cycling unit, buy a good trailer like the Cannondale Bugger.

There have been several different hitches for attaching the Bugger to the seat post of your bike. The earlier models tended to break or wear out until they slipped loose. The newer models, like the one shown in Illustration 38, have a much more sturdy and reliable design. Luckily, you can replace an old-style hitch with a new one. If you have the old style and want to modernize (this is the sort of low-tech modernization the world needs) you can get a new Bugger hitch from some of the large touring bike shops or from an extensive mail-order catalogue like the Cycl-ology one (see Addresses).

To attach the new hitch to your bike, first make sure the seat is up high enough (about 3½ inches) to accept the hitch easily. If the bike is the right size for you, the seat should be up at least that high. Push the hitch onto the post, then use two wrenches to tighten each bolt and nut. They can be tightened with one wrench, but the corners tend to get rounded off, and the holes get gouged out of shape if you don't use two tools.

The only tricks to loading the Bugger are balancing the load and holding things down well. Keep more weight toward the front of the trailer than to the back, or it will tend to tip backward and lift up the back of your bike whenever you get off it. You can use a box or homemade platform and bungee cords to hold big objects on your trailer. Small objects can be held on the canvas base with bungee cords, too. Local bike mechanic Dan Steiling has made a neat little wooden platform for his Bugger, and he takes both his luggage and his friendly dog, Fergie, wherever he goes. They take long tours as well as short trips around town. When Dan goes shopping, he can park the bike with the dog tied to the trailer and leave the whole unit unlocked. Fergie is as good a security system as you can buy, and he doesn't require a key or a combination! On long treks with heavy loads, Dan carries a leather harness for Fergie, and when they come to a long hill he hitches the dog up and they both pull the load to the mountaintop, shouting and barking encouragement to each other along the way up.

Maybe you don't have a dog team on tap to help you pull your loaded trailer up the steep hills. You may find that one problem with the trailer is that it works just fine with a heavy load *until* you get to a steep hill, but then starts playing tricks on you, like lifting the back wheel when you stand up to pedal or get off the bike, and rolling backward if you dismount without putting the brakes on. You have to learn to plan ahead. Get up a head of steam and shift into a lower gear *before* you hit the steeper grades, and put on the brakes and jump off the bike before it stops and starts to roll backward. On most normal grades, you can push the bike from the side, leaning on the seat if the trailer tries to tip up backward. If the load is really heavy and the grade is supersteep, you'll have to stand in front of the bike, facing backward, so you can hold the handlebars with both hands and lean backward to pull the load uphill. Keep your back straight as you lean, and use the strong muscles of your legs to do the work. Oh, it isn't easy. And the load must be balanced or it'll tip the trailer backward. But once you've learned the trick, and accepted the hard cold fact that you have to *work* to get up the steep hills, you can do it! Just don't get frustrated and quit after your first two or three difficult learning trips. Think of Dan and Fergie, riding up and down all the hills and mountains of California, undaunted by the slow climbs, yelping and hollering their way to the top of every one.

Going downhill, control your speed before it picks up, or the inertia will be too great for your brakes. You may even want to put heavy-duty brake pads on your bike for this reason (see page 10). Cornering must be done at lower speeds when you have a trailer, and you can never jerk suddenly to one side or the other. The trailer cannot lean into the turns; it will tip the other way and try to pull you that way too. Even if you manage to keep it upright, it will take a heavy beating as the centrifugal force pushes sideways on its wheels.

Keep the trailer wheels in mind when you're on bumpy roads, too. You have to plan for three wheel tracks instead of one. And if you can see that you can't get around a rock or pothole, hit it with your bike wheels rather than the trailer wheels. You can do some weight shifting on the bike. The trailer wheels smack into things without mercy, so you want to keep them clear of as many obstacles as possible.

Plan a good smooth route for regular trips you'll make with your trailer. It's even more important than route planning for a regular bike. You want to use those wide, newly paved streets and stay away from ones that have become minefields of patches and potholes, or ones where there isn't enough room for you to ride between the traffic and the curb or the parked cars. Narrow roads with lots of traffic and deep ditches at the edges are the worst. If one wheel of the trailer slips off the shoulder the trailer can tip suddenly and drag you into a bad fall.

Parking with a trailer is a bit harder than it is on a regular bike, but you can usually find a quiet corner or an isolated pole or tree to put your outfit next to. If the ground is sloped and the whole thing keeps trying to roll away, park the bike at an angle to the trailer, so both the back end and the front end of the whole unit are heading uphill. With the bike and trailer making a V opening uphill like that, neither can go anywhere. You can use a Flickstand on the front wheel of the bike to keep it from moving (see page 68), but the loaded trailer will be too heavy for the Flickstand to hold on anything but a very gentle grade. An alternative is to take a small bungee cord and wrap it around the down tube and the front wheel of the bike, locking the wheel in place just as the Flickstand does, but with more firmness.

There are a few alterations you can make on your Bugger trailer if you want it to be even lighter and better for long-distance rides. The first change many tourists make is to take off the wheels, clip all the spokes, and have a wheel builder rebuild the wheels using thin-profile 27-inch wheels and light tires like Specialized Bicycle Imports ones. For added strength, these wheels may be built on the type of hubs used for horse-drawn sulkies. These hubs fit the thick axle of the trailer and make for a very strong wheel that will carry almost any load, as long as you don't go smashing over ditches and boulders indiscriminately. Some people have tried to lace up the wheels with a dish, like the rear wheels on ten-speeds, so the rims will be as far out from the side of the trailer as possible. This means you won't have any trouble with the wheels scraping on the trailer, but it also weakens the wheels, and they will bend much more

Illustration **40**

easily when you hit bumps while going around curves. It's better to keep the rims centered, as on a normal front wheel, and don't load the trailer so heavily that the axle warps enough to make the tire hit the trailer side.

If you have two kids and neither of them is old enough to ride a bike alone, you can get a special Cannondale seat for your Bugger that will carry them in comfort, as long as they aren't bigger than about 50 pounds apiece. Pulling the 80-to-100-pound load uphill is grueling, to say the least, but if you are committed to using your pedal truck instead of a gas-gulping car, you can do it! The people of China and India have been carrying their families around on bikes for generations. If you come to a steep hill, just get the biggest kid out of the trailer and tell him or her to help push. That'll take some of the squirminess out of the little rascal.

There are other trailers than the classic Bugger, and some of the new ones may be well-suited to certain special purposes. So far, it seems to me that the quality and the versatility of the Cannondale Bugger has not been matched. If you are considering some other trailer, be especially wary of the ones that have flimsy or poorly-designed hitches. This is the part of the Bugger that works so well, after years of development. Also, make sure any trailer you buy has strong enough wheels and axles to handle the heaviest loads you can fit into it. If a trailer can hold a cubic yard of sand, it had better be built as strong as a contractor's wheelbarrow. I haven't seen any trailers that strong. To get a quick idea of the strength of any prospective trailer, just put a 50-pound sack of sand or a 50 pound kid in it and see what happens to the wheels and axles. If they bend so the tires hit the sides of the trailer, or if the frame seems to be unable to hold the weight, pass over the trailer and look for something stronger. If all you plan to do is make short, level trips to the grocery store on well-paved roads, you can get a simple plastic bucket trailer with fat balloon or semi-pneunatic tires. It won't look racy, and it won't feel very sporty, either, but it will get the job done.

Chapter 11
Balloon-tire Beauties

REMEMBER the dream bike of the forties and fifties? Its weight was in the forties or fifties, and it had tires that were so fat they could only hold about forty or fifty pounds pressure, but boy, if you got one for Christmas, especially one of those Schwinns with the bright and shiny paint jobs, you could zoom down the old driveway, pedals spinning, and imagine that you were going like sixty, even if you never did get up to even forty or fifty miles per hour.

The days when this bike dominated cycling are gone. But there are still good car-replacing uses for sturdy, wide-tired bikes, and there are excellent models still made by Schwinn and a number of small shops who have come up with superb special-purpose bikes such as the Moto-X racers and the light, multi-speed clunkers that can be ridden where no other bike dares venture.

The Ten-Block Bomber

This is the least elegant of the one-speed balloon-tire bikes. It is often called the "Balloon-tire Bomber" by those who remember the old days with affection. It will cover ten or twenty city blocks (even long blocks) with ease, especially if the terrain is flat. In San Francisco, bikes like the one shown in Illustration 41 are used to deliver parcels and mail down in the level business district. The riders hate taking things to addresses up on Nob Hill or Pacific Heights, but they get around fine where the streets are flat. Their thick tires bounce right over the cable car tracks, they can hop up and down curbs easily, they can carry lots of stuff in their big mailman-type baskets, and the bikes never get ripped off, either, They're too old and funky to be appealing to thieves.

. If you have an old bomber hanging around the back of your garage, or if you come across one in a garage sale and pick it up for a couple of bucks or so, you can fix it up for pennies and make all your short runs to the store on it. If you live close to work or to a mass transit station, you can ride it at least part way to and from work.

Illustration **41**   Ten Block Bomber

All you have to do to fix up the old bomber is get a set of nice new tires (they make lighter, easier-rolling ones now) and make sure the chain is oiled and at the correct, almost-tight setting. To get the chain set right, loosen the big rear wheel axle nuts, pull the wheel back in the frame (you may have to loosen the brake arm bolt and nut to do this), then tighten everything up thoroughly. Mounting a big mailman's sturdy basket on the bomber is a snap. You can get these baskets from most Schwinn bike shops or you can write a utility bike company like Worksman Cycles (see Addresses). Most bike catalogues don't carry them anymore, I'm sad to say.

There are lots of things you *don't* have to worry about if you have a decent balloon-tire bike. The gears don't slip, the brake cables don't break, the tires rarely go flat, and the bike won't be stolen unless you happen to live in an area where balloon-tire bombers have become a new fad. In the beach town where I live, the surfers have found out how useful a bomber is when riding with a surfboard under your arm, and a whole mystique has grown up around rusty Rollfasts and crumbling Columbias. If you have one of those fancy old Iversons with a spring-suspension front fork, you can't even leave it unguarded on the cliff while you go out surfing. It'll be ripped off by some greedy out-of-town gremlin for sure. At a recent flea market a broken-down Schwinn cowboy-style steed, complete with studs, fringe, and a demolished horn in the top tube tank was sold for fifty dollars to a bike dealer, who turned around and sold it to a collector for a hundred and fifty! Madness. I hope that sort of thing never starts in your neighborhood. With any luck you should be able to pick up a balloon-tire bike for less than twenty bucks, fix it up for another ten, and save a hundred or so on gas and car upkeep in the first year you use it. If you want to get a new balloon-tire bike, you'll have to pay four or five times as much as for an old one, but don't try to save a little by buying a cheap discount-store model. They're often poorly brazed or welded, so the frames don't hold up under the kind of rough use they always get. Get a good Schwinn if you can afford it. If you can't, get a bike that's got a reputation for being somewhere near as strong as the Schwinn.

If you want to fix up an old balloon-tire bike so it's really classy, you can take off the old beat-up pedals and put on new ones with reflectors (remember that the left pedal has backward threads, so you screw the old one out clockwise and the new one in counter-clockwise). Put a red reflector on the back of the seat or on the rear fender, and put a silver reflector on the front of the bike, for added safety. If you find that the gear on your bomber is either too high to get you up your local hills, or too low to get you going at a decent rate on the flat, you can change the gear by taking off the cranks and the front sprocket and putting on either a larger sprocket (for a higher gear) or a smaller sprocket (for a lower gear). You may have to add or take out a link in the chain; see a good bike manual if you don't know how to do the sprocket-changing or chain-altering procedures.

If the bike has one of those old padding-over-metal seats and the padding is frayed or half blown away, your fanny will hurt even after a short trip on the bike. There are excellent new seats you can use for comfort and style, as discussed on page 91. You don't need a seat with springs, though; your balloon tires will absorb most of the shocks the road doles out. Just get a nicely-shaped leather seat like the Ideale B6 or the Brooks B72 to make your short trips more pleasant.

Bikes for Young Riders

The best thing you parents can do for the future of transportation is to get a good bike for your young children today. Take the time to teach the kids how to ride correctly, then take rides together regularly, and you'll be able to watch your fledglings grow up without the total dependence on cars that we have all labored under.

Getting a good bike for your child is not easy. There are so many fads and cheap bikes made to take advantage of the fads. You have to find out what will work well for your child, then take a firm hand in deciding which bike will do the job. If a kid wants a Captain Blappy Bazooka Bike, complete with loop-de-loop handlebars, flame-red fake gas tank, and push-button death ray (batteries not included), steer the child toward a bike with a more usable riding position and a good, sturdy, no-frills frame. The flashy bikes for kids that are sold at many discount stores often have poorly-built frames, weak wheels, and cheap flaky paint jobs. They break, bend, and rust away in a matter of months, giving the young consumer a first strong taste of planned obsolescence. Of course, next year's model comes out, with Colonel Clobber's Cloning Cyclotron (4 BEV klystron tubes not included), but you can avoid the whole sickening treadmill by starting with a simple, well-built machine. If you want a clear idea of what a sturdy child's bike looks like, go see a Schwinn dealer. The prices will seem outrageous, but at least you can take a close look at bicycles with strong frames, sturdy wheels, and fantastic paint jobs that will last under even the most rambunctious child's treatment.

If you go hunting for a cheaper brand than the standard-setting Schwinn, you may find numerous bikes that are not only cheaper but lighter than the Schwinns. There are a few of these lighter bikes that work fine, at least for a beginning rider. We had one very light AMF bike for five years, and it went through two sons and many oversize neighborhood borrowers before it finally broke in half. In fact, it was even used when we bought it. Children's bikes of all makes show up in flea markets and garage sales. They usually have a bent wheel or a bashed pedal or two, but you can either hunt down other used parts, or get new ones from a bike shop in order to get the used bike running like new.

Illustration **42**

Learning
Two-Wheel Balance

Make sure you get a bike with a SMALL frame, whether it's a new or used bike. A fourteen-inch frame (you measure from the center of the bottom bracket axle, where the pedals revolve in the frame, to the top of the seat tube, where the seat post slides down into the frame) will be more than big enough for most five-to-eight-year-old riders. For even younger beginners, consider getting a tiny sidewalk bike with little semi-pneumatic tires and pedals that are connected by the chain directly to the rear wheel. These are only safe on flat sidewalks and driveways, though, so as soon as the child gets to the exploring-beyond-the-backyard stage, buy a bike with balloon tires and a coaster brake.

The wheels and tires must be sturdy. They will take a thorough beating. If you live in town, the bike will jump off, run up, and smash into many curbs in its life. If you live out in the country, the wheels will fly over dirt-clods, potholes, logs, and river stones, not to mention a stray dog or cat now and then. So get wheels with good thick spokes, wide, squared-off rims (not those skimpy ones with the V cross section) and sturdy tires with thick treads. Keep the tires *fully* inflated at all times; it'll save you a lot of rim work.

Another stitch that'll save you nine is keeping the wheels and wheel bearings adjusted and bolted on tight. If a wheel gets loose in the frame, tighten the big axle nuts thoroughly. If the wheel is loose on its bearings, tighten up the left-side axle nut (on the rear wheel this is the side with the brake arm). Then loosen the big axle nut on the right side of the wheel, loosen the bearing locknut if there is one around the axle inside the frame dropout, then adjust the bearings so the wheel rolls smoothly but doesn't have any free play from side to side. Tighten the locknut if there is one, then tighten the big axle nut and check to make sure the wheel still rolls smoothly. Don't ever fool with the left side of a coaster brake hub. If adjusting the bearings doesn't help a noisy, sticky, or slipping coaster-brake hub, work a little oil into it, and if that doesn't help, take the rear wheel off the bike and give it to a good bike shop that has an old-fashioned, dyed-in-the-wool coaster brake expert and have the hub rebuilt. It's not that big a job, but it has to be done right, and with the correct parts. Old pros are best at making sure your new brake parts work in your old hub.

The handlebars and seats on many kid's bikes are terrible. Banana seats with flimsy tin supports and flashy plastic cushions are not only tasteless but dangerous. They encourage double-riding, which novice cyclists shouldn't try, and their weak supports always come loose, break, or collapse. As for those huge ape-hanger handlebars, they are so dangerous that many states have outlawed them completely. Even the imitation motorcycle bars, the ones with the wide ends and the brace across the top, make it hard for a small rider to control the bike. If your kid insists that those Moto-X bars are a must, you should take him or her to a shop that sells stuff for the really competitive Moto-X racers, and have a look at the light little bars they put on their racing machines. BMX racers, like competitors in all sports, have found out that the smaller, lighter, more utilitarian equipment is the best. Their bars never reach up and out more than is comfortable, and they use small, light racing bicycle saddles instead of those flimsy banana seats. So start your child out on a bike with a small, sturdy saddle and a pair of bars that are either flat (like a miniature version of the bars on an adult three-speed) or sticking up and out only a bit (such as the bars on the BMX racing bikes).

Set the bike up so it fits the kid. If it's a small child, put the seat down as far as it will go, and set the handlebars low, too. If you've got the Moto-X type, loosen the binder bolt on the stem and twist the bars back a bit, so the kid can reach them easily, then tighten them firmly in that position.

Helping a young person learn to ride a bike for the first time is easier than you'd think. First, see if he or she can easily reach the ground while sitting on the bike seat. If the bike's way too big for that, DON'T try to make the kid learn on it. Get a smaller bike or wait until the kid grows up. If the child can reach the ground with both feet, but not easily, take the pedals off the bike. Why? Because the best way to learn to ride a bike is to coast on it at first, without trying to propel it at all. You don't have to hold the bike for your child, or provide any complicated instructions at all. Kids love coasting around on little wheeled toys. They'll get into riding down the sidewalk on their new two-wheeler right away, and in a couple of days they'll learn to push and balance their way along on their toes, whooping it up like hyenas on parade. The only danger is that they may find a big hill somewhere and launch themselves down it without any idea of how to STOP their speedy new coasters.

Keep an eye on your budding cyclist to avoid such a mishap, and when you feel that she or he has got the balance down, put the pedals back onto the bike and teach the kid how the brakes work before you even get into pedaling forward in order to pick up speed. At the early braking and pedaling stage, you may have to spend a little time trotting around holding the back of the bike to keep it balanced while the child concentrates on steering and doing things with the pedals. Don't let the little rascal con you into being the motor and balancer for more than a day or so. Kids will balance and use the pedals right when they're ready to. They don't need any pushing, in most cases, especially if they see older kids riding around the neighborhood and want to get into the act.

So your child can learn to balance, pedal, and brake the bike without much trouble on your part. But that's only the first part of learning how to ride a bike. The other part is much harder. It takes much more time and effort, and is frustrating and scary for any parent. It is the business of teaching your child to ride safely. There are no biker education courses offered in schools that come anywhere near the quality of safety training that people get when they get ready to take a driver's license test. So you, the parent, have to take charge.

The best approach, I think, is to take your child on as many short local bike trips as possible. You ride your bike, your kid rides his or her bike alongside. You can go to and from school this way, if the school isn't too far away. You can make runs to the store and the kid can even take a little backpack and help carry stuff home. If he or she is dying to have an ice cream, ride bikes to the ice cream parlor some afternoon. Or if the bambino wants to go to a nearby friend's house, go via bike. In many cases, the other kid will not have a bike, but you can carry this friend on your child seat and still do any trips they want to do together.

On every bike trip such as those mentioned, WATCH the traffic and WATCH your kid, every foot of the way. Concentrate on teaching the basic safety rules, such as riding as far to the right as possible (maybe the kid should even ride on the road shoulder or the sidewalk to begin with), stopping or slowing down almost to a stop at intersections so you can look all around for cars, signalling when turning, riding in a straight line instead of weaving and jumping off every curb in sight, things like that. And make sure your kid gets a clear idea of the importance of keeping eyes and ears open for cars at all times. A little dose of courtesy might be good at this time, too. Letting cars and pedestrians pass at intersections, making good eye contact with drivers, all of those little things that combine safety with road decency, thus building up the image of the good cyclist.

There will certainly be a few scares in spite of all the teaching and encouragement you give your child. We all have our lapses of concentration, and kids have a much greater tendency to be distracted by things like a ball they are chasing, a butterfly they want to catch, or a friend they are trying to beat in a race. Just be thankful that more close calls don't turn into accidents, and that most accidents are minor. When a close call or minor fall does happen, however, make sure the child realizes just how dangerous the situation was. What was a bad experience can turn into a good learning one.

It's incredible that more kids aren't hit by cars. They seem to be protected by some magic good angel. Give that angel all the help you can, so the next generation can grow up in one piece, with a keen sense for both the joy and the responsibility of cycling.

Hot Rod Clunkers and Moto-X Bikes

Both of these types of bikes have grown out of the classic balloon-tire bombers, but they have grown into very, very different machines, made for different purposes.

Hot Rod Clunkers are for either zooming around town in style, or tearing down mountain trails with wild abandon. I like zooming down mountain trails, but I prefer to do it on a light, sensitive bike. Clunkers lend themselves to uncontrollable speeds, power slides, and the creation of deep erosion gullies on sharp turns. It's fun, but it carves up the hillsides, and I don't approve of that. As for cruising around town on a clunker, it makes more sense to me than cruising in a hot rod 4-wheel-drive pickup, but much less than riding around town on a lightweight bicycle like the good old three-speed. So I'm not going to go into great detail about how to rig up a first-class clunker bike. Some of the most commonly used materials are wide, braced Moto-X-type handlebars; strong but lightweight gear changers and cotterless cranks, borrowed from ten-speed racers; disc or drum hub brakes like the ones used on tandems; wheels with thick (11- or 12-gauge) spokes, light steel or aluminum rims, and balloon tires with either narrow cross section (to keep the

Illustration **43**   Joe Breeze Bike

weight down) or extra-fat cross section (for riding in mud, sand, or dust). Superfancy brazed frames are made by a few craftsmen such as Joe Breeze of Marin County, California. He puts things like Campagnolo seat posts, cantilever brakes, and sealed-hub wheels on his frames. The final product is definitely for the fanatic fringe. If you've got lots of money and dreams of riding the John Muir Trail from one end to the other, you might look into a hot ballooner. Otherwise, you'd do better to stick with more standard equipment.

Moto-X bikes go off in another direction. They are built for big-time competition. There's a thrill to it, with the burst of speed, the sliding corners, the flying dust and mud. As long as the adults don't get too heavy-handed about making sure their kid WINS, young riders can have lots of fun racing. Because of the heavy competition, though, bike Moto-X has gone far beyond the realm of the old Schwinn sting-ray we used for torching around in empty parking lots.

The frame of the typical racing machine will be of arc-welded chrome molybdenum steel, and it will cost a bundle. It will have a gusset (flat brace) or double gussets at the joint of the head, top, and down tubes, and it will be quick, light (in the 3–5-pound range), and sturdy. There aren't many brazed Moto-X frames around, but some are made, using the methods of road-racing frame construction. The forks on a BMX bike are not usually light, because of the fact that they must take such a severe beating. They are made of thick chrome-molly tubes. A heavy upper column meets or bisects an upside-down U-shape with no rake other than the offset of the dropouts, which are attached to the front side of the forks. Such forks are about as responsive as the front end of a Mack truck.

The cranks and bottom bracket units are like those used on road-racing bikes, or they may be modified with a nylon chainwheel. There are special adapting kits, available from the better BMX shops or big catalogues like Cycl-ology (see Addresses), for putting a ten-speed-type axle and bearings in an American wide-diameter bottom bracket shell. Some of the fancy frames are made with a ten-speed-size shell, into which you can put sealed bearings just like the road racers use. These sealed bearings are very expensive, but you never have to replace them because of dirt damage.

The wheels for Moto-X bikes are very specialized. Light alloy rims, thick spokes (11-, 12-, or 14-British gauge; 120-, 105-, or 80-American gauge), and road-racing hubs with either high or low flanges are used. To me, low-flange hubs make more sense; they have a bit more give, and absorb shocks better. The supple willow bends where breaks the mighty oak. Either type of hub with a tension-spoked wheel is more resilient than the mag or nylon compression-spoked wheel. These latter types are not common among racers. The rear wheel usually has a freewheel, or in some cases, two freewheels, one for each side of the wheel (on a flip-flop-type hub). Having two gear choices is great when you go from one type of track to another, but the option jacks up the price of the wheel by about a third.

Many production bikes have a foot brake for the rear hub, but lots of race models have opted for the lightness and better control you can get from a sturdy side-pull caliper brake. Most of the better frames come with a brake bridge between the seat stays, and a hole drilled in the bridge just for the brake mechanism. Use a sturdy brake handle, such as the Dia-Compe Moto-X model or the large types found on mopeds. If you have small hands, the Dia-Compe bent handle will work best on standard Moto-X handlebars, lining up with the grips so you can reach the brake easily. The brake cable housing should be stainless steel and the cable should be the Campagnolo woven type, or something equally strong, to put up with the punishment of dirt riding.

The brake mechanism should be a side-pull one that is strong and simple. Some of the fancier brake mechanisms, such as the Campagnolo and others like it, have a long, delicate upper extension on the brake arm that holds the end of the cable housing. This delicate brake arm sticks out there like an invitation to passing bushes, rocks, and other bikes to smash into. Some of the cheaper side-pull brakes have shorter brake arm extensions, and although this gives you a little less leverage, the brakes will last longer. They work fine if you keep them adjusted right and work on your right-hand grip muscles so you can squeeze the handle hard enough when you need to slow down fast, like when the whole pack goes into a pile-up right in front of you.

For superpositive braking, consider the low-priced Shimano cantilever brakes. Adult cyclo-cross racers have used Mafac cantilever brakes for years, but the Mafacs have long cantilever arms that stick out to the sides of the bike even more than the Campy brake arms. The Shimano cantilever system has a sturdier, more streamlined design, and still delivers excellent braking power, even when the wheels are wet, covered with mud, or bent all wobbly. The only trouble with the Shimano brakes is that the cantilever posts have to be brazed to the seat stays. This is not easy; it must be done by a real brazing expert, so the brakes get brazed on there for good without the metal getting so heated up that the bike frame is weakened. If you can't find a first-rate metalworking shop to put your cantilevers on, stick with the standard side-pull brakes, and take an extra brake mechanism to races with you in case you smash one in a race.

The seat on a Moto-X bike should be small, light, and strong. Leather won't hold up in mud and dust, so use a nylon seat such as the Unicanitor or cheaper Taiwan copies. It should be held on a post that will not slip at all. The best and lightest one around is the S.R. (Sakae, from Japan) model of the French

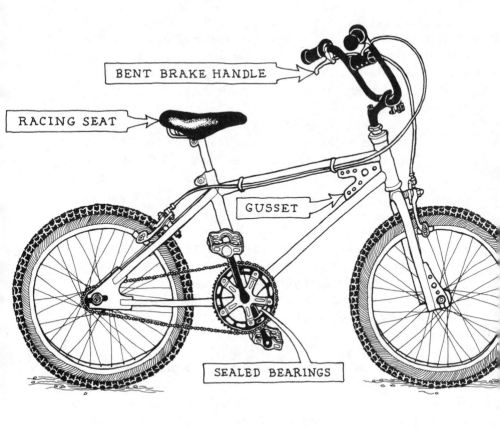

BENT BRAKE HANDLE

RACING SEAT

GUSSET

SEALED BEARINGS

Illustration **44** Moto-X Bike

Laprade seat post. It isn't that expensive, it's lighter than most
other seat posts, it's easy to adjust to whatever position you
want, and it will hold up under the most brutal punishment.
The only trouble with the S.R. Laprade post is that it's not very
long. You tall riders will need the big 15-inch post with the
strongest seat clamp you can get your hands on. The post
should be held in the frame by a heavy-duty clamp, too. Special
alloy ones with two bolts are sold, but the standard design will
work fine if the metal is strong and the single bolt is tightened
thoroughly.

Moto-X handlebars are changing. They used to be high and
wide, a cross between the old ape-hanger bars and the widest
type of motorcycle "trial" bars. But the high and wide bike bars
are made more for showing off (wheelies, jumps, etc.) and for

controlling slides, rather than for speed. As Moto-X competition has stiffened, riders have found that smaller, lighter bars are better for going fast. As this has happened, they have found that the old problem of the bars coming loose in the stem has gotten much less serious. I wouldn't be surprised if in the near future they start using bars that look almost like the old all-rounder ones. This type of bar can be raised up on a strong stem like the Tuff Neck, or you might even be able to get by with a superstrong standard type stem. As the handlebars get smaller, the forks take less abuse, too. If a rider refrains from Evel Knievel jumps, a well-brazed chrome-molly fork such as the double-plate crown ones used by the champion cyclo-cross racers might suffice.

Now, with a light, responsive front end like the one described above, kids might be able to show more finesse while sliding through turns and accelerating down straights through traffic. I'd love to see a little more finesse in the sport, and a lot less of the typical buffalo stampede that always leads to pile-ups, injuries, tears, and the survival of the meanest. Oh well, finesse might go against the spirit of the sport, as most people see it. All I can say is that I've done a lot of riding and racing in the mud, and the supple, light, and graceful bikes often prevail where the buffaloes bog down. And it's more fun to ride with finesse.

One last word from an old mud runner. Don't spend too much money on pedals. You're going to ruin them no matter how good they are. Get good plastic sleeve-bearing pedals or metal ball-bearing rat-trap pedals that are contoured for ground clearance. They're plenty strong and cost about one-quarter the price of the best sealed-bearing MX pedals. The cheap ones will break if you really slam into them, but then so will the fancy ones, and if you break a cheap one, at least you won't have lost all that money, so you'll be able to replace them more easily. By the way, always take extra pedals to races; if you check your pedals between heats and find one that's starting to fall apart, you can change it in time for the next heat.

The best technique for bike Moto-X racing is simple. Go like hell when the gate drops. If you can take the lead before the first turn or as you go through the first turn, you'll almost surely win the heat. Make sure you have a gear that is right for the start of the course (higher if it's a downhill start, lower if it's level), and have your starting pedal high and your foot ready to jump down on it. As you practice starts (and you must do more of that kind of practice than any other) concentrate on delivering as much power to the rear wheel as you can without flailing and wobbling around. Of course, if you gain the lead, it may help to move across the track, back and forth, to keep the riders from getting past you, but even this should be done smoothly. If you're wobbling, you're losing energy and taking a risk of a DQ (disqualification) for bumping another rider. In any contact situation, it's the wild, flailing rider who gets the DQ, whereas the smooth rider is assumed innocent.

Smoothness over obstacles is critical, too. Showy jumps are slower than quick slithers over the bumps. Stand up off the saddle, keep your arms and legs bent so they absorb the shock, and keep the rear wheel on the ground, so it can keep accelerating. On flat or off-camber hairpin turns, the showy, long slide is much slower than the short, braking slide that drops you into the perfect line for maximum speed through a curve. You can make a single stab at the ground with your inside foot at the apex of a real sharp turn, then start a quick jump of acceleration as you come out of the hole, with NO sliding or peeling out, so you can get up to peak speed quickly in the straightaway. A really great rider can come at a corner from wide, quick-slide right into the tightest fast line, and pass a slower, sloppy-sliding rider on the inside; then increase the lead by taking that one foot-punch to stop the slide, get balance, and begin the break out of the hole.

Remember the flying finish, too. Even if you don't have a chance for first place, go for it. It looks much better, and the other riders may have a freak fall or something, especially if they are fighting it out for first place. If the leaders go down, you've got to be right there and going your fastest to take advantage of the break. So go full-out, all the way, in every Moto.

Chapter 12
High Speed Bikes: Less Is More

THE WORLD of ultralight, ultrafast ten-speed bicycles is glutted with specialization and high prices. If you want to get the lightest possible bike for your purposes, first make sure you know exactly what you're going to do with the bike, then buy just the equipment that's made for your bike and riding style.

For instance, it makes no sense at all to buy a superlight time-trial frame, with all kinds of titanium equipment, then use wheels with heavy clincher tires because you can't be bothered with sew-ups. Nor does it make any sense to get a really stiff, snappy Criterium racing frame with head angles of about 75 degrees, and then try to rig the thing up for a tour over the cobblestone roads of Europe. If you don't understand the difference between the frames mentioned above, DON'T go hunting for the perfect superlight bike without consulting a reliable expert who knows your riding tastes and skills. You can read up on frame and equipment terms in books like *Bike Tripping*, by myself and Albert Eisentraut, but to be up on the latest high-tech equipment that's being put out for cycling high-rollers, you need to be an aerospace engineer and a pro racer at the same time.

Some general hints will help to guide you if you want to just start with a nice, light, well-made standard frame, and get reasonably light equipment for your needs.

First off, spend the bulk of your bike budget on the frame and wheels. Get a frame that has a reputation for strength and lightness, one that's made for general road use, unless you already have a bike that covers all your standard needs and you need one for some new specialty you are very serious about. For normal road riding, get a frame with 72–73 degree head and seat tube angles, a fork with about 50 mm (2 in.) of rake, a length (or wheelbase, measured from dropout to dropout) of 100 to 105 centimeters and either double-butted or light straight-gauge chrome-molybdenum or high-grade high-carbon steel. Tange, Columbus, and Reynolds have made first-rate tubes for most of the world's great bike frames. Other companies come close to or equal the quality of the three leaders though,

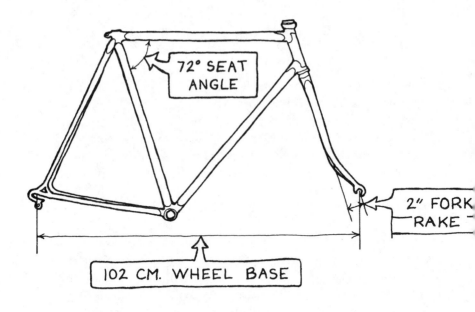

Illustration 45   General-use Frame Design

so don't turn down a bike just because it doesn't have tubes made by one of the big three. Once you've got a good, light frame for your bike, the other parts can be fair to middling, and the thing will still perform quite well.

The wheels do have to be good in order for the bike to ride comfortably, though. Start with the best hubs you can afford. Campagnolo sets the standard, but others are fine, too. Sealed bearing hubs are a good idea if you ride in wet weather a lot. Low flange hubs will be the best for general purposes, and are fine for most types of road racing as well. Get strong, light aluminum alloy rims, such as those made by Super Champion. Rims have changed a great deal in the past few years, and you may have to wade through a lot of mixed advice when you go shopping for rims. In general, rims with a hollow cross section can give you the best weight-strength ratio, as long as the alloy is high grade. Both clincher and sew-up rims are made with a wide variety of designs these days. For normal road riding, a strong 350-gram sew-up rim or a 475-gram clincher rim (like the

Rainbow or the Gentleman by Super Champion) will be strong enough for all but the heaviest riders. The wheels should be laced up with strong spokes, either zinc-plated rustless or very high-grade stainless ones like those made by DT of Switzerland. They may be butted, like the DT 14-15-14 (British Wire Gauge) spokes, but if you can't get those, make sure you get ones that are strong enough for your intended use. Saving half an ounce of weight on spokes at the expense of keeping your wheels together makes no sense at all.

The spokes should be laced so they touch at the cross that's closest to the rim, and for normal road use they should be three-cross. That means that if you start at the head of any spoke and follow it out to the rim, it will pass over or under three other spokes.

After getting light, strong wheels and a spiffy frame for your bike, concentrate on the crankset, including the bottom bracket. The cranks should be aluminum alloy, cotterless, and matched with as light a bottom bracket set as you can get for your money. The classic cranks are made by Campagnolo, but there are many others that will work as well and cost much less. Shimano, Sugino, Stronglight, and the bargain-priced Sakae (SR) cranks are almost all good enough for normal use. If they are mounted carefully, using a little grease between the square end of the axle and the square hole in each crank, they will go together smoothly and never come loose. Tighten each crank bolt slowly, and retighten them every 25 miles or so during the first few hundred miles of use. This will ensure that the cranks are seated well, where they will stay put even after they are broken in. There are many different bottom bracket sets, ranging from the superlight OMAS titanium set, to the roller-bearing models, to the sealed sets such as the one made by Phil Wood. To me, the Phil Wood unit is the best because it is fairly light (about 280 grams) and impervious to dust, water, and long hard use. I know that because mine has gone through every kind of madness and mud, and it still works perfectly!

All of the other things you put on your bike are less critical. If you can get good aluminum alloy parts, like a Black-burn rear carrier, a light water bottle cage, light handlebars, stem, seat, and seat post, it may make a difference of a pound or more in the total weight of the bike. If you're the kind of person who can't resist fancy goodies for your bike, and you have Campy or Campy-size components now, you might get the titanium bolts and nuts kit that OMAS of Italy makes. It costs about four or five times the price of the standard parts kit, but it cuts the weight in half, making for a saving of about half a pound in most cases.

Then there are things like superlight pure latex clincher inner tubes, aluminum spoke nipples, and aluminum brake cable housing. These all have real drawbacks. The cable housings flex too much, the spoke nipples strip out, and the latex inner tube seeps air so fast you have to pump it up twice a day. Your bike will work fine without those things, and the difference of weight isn't worth the trouble. As for the ultimate in less weight for more money, the titanium chain, BAH, *HUMBUG!* I'll stick with my Sedis, at about one-twentieth the price. If I eat a little less breakfast before a ride, I'll save as much as the weight difference, and save a hundred and forty bucks in the process. I mean, just because Eddy Merckx did things like filling his tires with helium for his hour attempt in Mexico doesn't mean that you and I should go to drastic extremes for every ride we take around the block.

While I'm on this tirade, I've gotta take a cut at drilling, too. If you want to buy drilled-out parts, like brake levers and chainwheels, you can go right ahead. They look neat even if they don't save you much weight. But unless you know all about fulcrums, cantilevers, and the limits of shearing stress, don't use your own hand drill to turn your bike into Swiss cheese. Swiss cheese has this floppy, fragile nature that doesn't go along with the idea of strong bicycle equipment. Leave your alloy bike parts as they are, or buy new ones that have been designed and drilled by experts if your heart is set on the filigree look.

If you have light sew-up or clincher tires, you may even want to *add* one small bit of weight to the bike to keep flats to a minimum. Tire savers are little curved pieces of wire held by your brake mounting bolts so they graze along the surface of the tires and snag out anything that gets stuck in them. They pull out thorns, tacks, and glass shards before the sharp debris works through the tire casing into the tube. They work fine if you keep them bent to just the right shape, but the sound they make is bothersome. They hiss against the tire wherever there is any slight variation in the roundness of the wheel, and this sound gets on your nerves when you're cruising along some quiet, lovely road trying to listen to birds, the wind, and nice things like that. But if you can put up with the noise, you can use tire savers and save lots of flats.

No gadget can take all the risk out of riding a superlight road machine, though. You have to accept the delicateness of your light bike and treat it with respect. Ride on smooth roads as much as possible, and don't ride at night if you can help it. Hitting a big rock or running into an unseen chuckhole in the dark can pop a tire, bend a tire rim, or even collapse a light-weight frame.

This is especially true if you weigh a lot yourself. Bikes made in the European tradition of racing are intended for riders who weigh less than 160 pounds. If you weigh over 175, you'll need some equipment that's stronger and a bit heavier than the ultralight stuff. Get a rim that's made for strength, even if it is 50–100 grams heavier than its superlight counterpart. Use strong rustless straight-gauge spokes, or the very strongest stainless spokes made by DT of Switzerland. You may even opt for a 40-spoke rear wheel, just for added safety. Get a sturdy tire, too, with a relatively wide profile, to support your wide profile. The Clement Del Mundo is the classic tubular or sew-up tire for this purpose. The Specialized Bicycle Imports Touring tire is a great wide-profile clincher, and there are others at comparable or even lower prices.

You can have a much lighter front wheel, but don't cut corners on the rear one or you'll always be patching, straightening, or respoking it. To me, the extra weight of a strong rear wheel isn't so bothersome, anyway. If my front wheel is light and responsive, my steering feels quick and lively, so the whole feel of the bike is good. I just keep my eyes and mind on that light front wheel and thank my stars that I don't have many flats or wheel problems with my tough-but-hefty back unit.

Use good riding technique when you're on your light road bike. It'll save you lots of damage to your special equipment. The key is to ride smoothly. Don't lunge from side to side as you stand up on the pedals to power up a hill. Imagine that your head is on a string that runs a straight line in your direction of travel. You'll find that if you keep your head still, the rest of your body will pump and rotate in a balanced, coordinated flow, so you're never wrenching the bike frame and wheels with lots of sloppy sideways motion. By the way, you waste less energy when you ride smoothly like that. All the dramatic flailing and lunging young racers do is a big waste of power. The idea is to make the bike jump *forward* when you accelerate, not sideways. Very few races are won on bikes going sideways.

Your braking and cornering should be as even-handed as your smooth pedaling technique. Use both brakes as you approach a curve. Let out on the front one a bit sooner than the rear as you feel the centrifugal force pull you in the curve. Use leaning more than sharp jerks of the handlebar to turn. The straight line your head follows when pedaling should become a beautiful, smooth curve around each corner, dipping low, but no lower than necessary. Pedal hard, but with complete smoothness as you come out of a sharp corner. If there is any gravel, sand, or dust on the surface, or if it's wet, don't pedal or brake so hard, and pick a "line" or path through the turn that takes into account the poor surface conditions and avoids the worst patches of slippery stuff.

Stay off raggedy roads with lots of chuckholes, or ride very slowly on them. Don't ever ride on jeep trails or creek beds. Even a dirt road that seems soft and gentle may have a hidden rock or root that you will hit with your front wheel. Also, it only takes one loose stick to jam your wheels or ruin your derailleur.

If you go touring on your superlight bike, pack as lightly as possible, and make sure you follow the method of balancing the load described on page 56. If there is too much weight in one place, like over the back wheel, you're going to have spoke and tire problems back there. For carrying light loads, a Blackburn rear rack and a little handlebar pack should be plenty. Obviously, you can't take much camping gear, or even a big sleeping bag. You have to use hostels, hotels, or friends' houses instead.

There is another whole frontier of light-and-fast cycling that doesn't get much attention because you don't see the bikes around every day. This is the realm of the man-powered speed-record vehicles. You can't call them bicycles because many have three, four, or even more wheels. They are often covered with streamlined shells, and they are mainly for riding in a long straight line, accelerating to top speed as they go through electronic "traps" or timing lights.

Due to the heroic efforts of bike-speed nuts like Dr. Chester Kyle, Allan Abbott, and Paul Van Valkenburgh, there is an official event to determine just how fast a human being can propel him- or herself. This may seem like a frivolous race, since the vehicles aren't much good for doing anything *but* going fast in a straight line, but the race is significant for two reasons.

For one thing, it is a known fact that a man riding a bicycle is the most efficient form of transportation on earth. More efficient than any animal or any other machine that man has made. In these energy-starved times, we should be aware of any experiment that is aimed at increasing the efficiency of the most efficient form of transportation around. We might learn some very, very significant things from those Gyro Gearloose machines that zoom down the flat track in Ontario, California every spring. They're onto something that could be big some day, even if Detroit and Madison Avenue have ignored them until now.

More significant for the common bike rider than the records being set at the cutting edge of man-powered speed, there are designs coming from some of the competitors that may soon find their way onto the streets. Among the modern entries in the International Human Powered Speed Championships at Ontario there have been several designs that could be modified into fast, easily-controlled street vehicles. The Gentes "Silver Bullet", which placed third in the hour attempt and fifth in the road race in 1979, was great on the corners as well as on the straight flat course. This versatility is important if the design is to gain acceptance on the road. A supine bicycle made by Gardner Martin and Nathan Dean, similar to their stream-lined racer, is now used by family and friends to do errands and commuting. A hand-foot powered "Manuped", which is very fast on the track, has also been adapted to street use. In a recent English competition, an enclosed recumbent bicycle with small wheels and the pedals in front of the front wheel (made by W. G. Lydiard) showed great promise as a city vehicle.

The first of these machines, the Silver Bullet, could be used as-is for fairly long rides. It has an exotic steering mechanism, but it can be mastered in a matter of minutes. The other three machines are sensitive to crosswinds when they have their streamlined bodies on. If you try to turn them into a strong side wind, you have to lean so far the bodies hit the ground and the bikes tip over. But the power-efficient Manuped and the stalwart Martin and Dean supine recumbent (they call it the Easy Racer or "chopper" because it looks like one of those chopped Harleys) can be used without cumbersome fairings. They aren't as fast that way, but they still make for much less wind resistance than the tall standard bikes.

I rode an Easy Racer around and found it quite easy to get used to, as long as you don't try to make a sharp turn while riding slowly. The bike is so long and the front fork is set at such a radical angle that you can't turn as sharp as you want to when balancing and maneuvering at low speeds. Once you get going, though, it steers and balances like a dream. It's a joy to zoom along at 20 miles per hour or so, with only about half the wind resistance you would have on a normal bike. The stability in high-speed curves is phenomenal; your low center of gravity makes you feel much more secure as you tuck down into a turn and whoosh through it.

Illustration **46** A   **Easy Racer Recumbent**

And you *are* more secure. If you fall or run into something on a supine recumbent bike like the Easy Racer or Manuped, your feet are out in front of you, so you can cushion the impact with your legs, or sit down on your backside padding. Compare this with the way you fly head-first into any accident on a standard ten-speed, and the Easy Racer starts to look pretty attractive. It isn't so easy to park as standard bikes, and you may feel vulnerable in traffic unless you put an orange flag on your recumbent, but you have to admit, these bikes perform beautifully. The Martin and Dean machine is made from standard bicycle materials, too, so it could easily be mass-produced without high-tech materials or machines. The speedier Manuped recumbent would be harder to produce inexpensively, due to its complex design.

Recumbent bikes won't suit everyone, either. The pedaling position can get to your knees if the bike isn't just the right size for you. But if you could ride an Easy Racer that fits you, as I did, you might just fall in love with the thing. I hope recumbents like the Martin and Dean bike or the Manuped will soon become available to the general public.

In the meantime, let's hope all the inventors of tomorrow's

Illustration 46B   Streamlined Recumbent

human-powered vehicles can keep up the good work, and get more support from government and investors. The standard superlight bikes of today work well, but they are *not* the perfect, final answer to the challenge of pedal transport. And if there is one thing we can rely on to find better cycling answers for tomorrow, it's Yankee ingenuity. The Wright Brothers, Henry Ford, and many lesser inventors got started in bike shops. Who knows, the future of cycling may be under development in some cluttered garage, right now!

Chapter 13
Portable Bikes—For Travel in Two Modes

SOMETIMES YOU can't do your whole trip on a bike. If you have to cover lots of distance in a short period of time, or if you have to go through a major city every day during rush hour, or if you have to cross a mountain range, or an ocean or something, you need to take a faster, more powerful mode of transportation. But you don't have to leave your bike behind. You can get a nifty fold-up bike and take it along, and when you get over the mountain or the ocean and alight from the other mode of transit (let's hope it's a *mass transit* vehicle, so you're at least saving energy by traveling in a group) you can put the bike together, hop on, and ride away, a happy cyclist again.

There are some useable porta-bikes on the market, and there will probably be others coming out soon. Far and away the most unusual and most famous is the Bickerton, which looks like a kid's bike with giraffe tendencies, but which is light and quite easy to use, both when riding and carrying. There are other fold-up type bikes with more conventional construction, such as the Di Blasi of Italy and the heavier Raliegh fold-up Twenty, but these are harder to find either because they are sold only by small importing firms, or because they are out of production altogether.

There is a great new American machine, the Pocket Bicycle, conceived of by the proprietors of the Hub and Axle Bicycle Company, E. Hubbard Yonkers and Sven Axle Tullborg. The bike is lovingly and painstakingly crafted by Dave Hartranft of Cambridge, Massachusetts, and it gets raves from everyone who sees and rides it. The Pocket Bike is made of both the finest Reynolds 531 tubing and the strongest wide-diameter chrome-molybdenum steel tubes. It also depends on stainless steel tension cables for strength. The cables form a diamond around the crossed frame tubes and are tightened to give the bike much more rigidity and structural stability than any of the other folding bikes. Experts find the Pocket Bike even more stable than many full-size machines! Not since the Dursley-Pederson of the early 1900s has there been a machine that so elegantly uses tension and triangulation to make a high-performance bicycle.

Illustration 47 Portable Pocket Bicycle

The Pocket Bike folds up into a package that is bigger than the folded Bickerton, but it doesn't weigh much more, and it is much easier to fold and unfold, as well as ride.

Alas, the Pocket Bicycle is very expensive. Even if you are willing to pay the price, which is more than double that of the Bickerton and standard road bikes, you have to wait while the slow and meticulous maker finishes your bike. If you want the best, you'll pay and wait. There is talk of mass-producing a cheaper but heavier version of the Pocket Bicycle, and we all look forward to its debut. In the meantime, if you want to inquire about the present machine, see Addresses.

The Bickerton folding bicycle isn't a high performance machine (it has a wild "wet-noodle" feel to it), and its design is anything but elegant, but it *is* available. It can be found in some specialty shops around the country, and in some of the better catalogues (see Addresses). It is the whimsical invention of a backyard wizard, Harry Bickerton. It comes with an owner's manual, written by Harry himself. The first part of this manual is one of the greatest bits of "how-to" literature ever written. It has to be. The bike is so confusing that you must rely heavily on the book to survive your first attempt at unfolding the machine. The thing is, you have to get to know and respect the personalities of both Harry and his bike if you are going to use the machine seriously. If you're even vaguely considering buying a Bickerton, go to a shop that carries it, or seek out another cyclist who has one, and just read the first pages of Harry's manual.

You'll love it. If you're a tinkerer like me, you'll fall in love with the bike, too. Don't get too romantic about it, though. It is just a bike, after all, and it has very real weaknesses. If you don't keep them in mind, you can get into a good deal of trouble. I remember one day I was helping a friend fix his

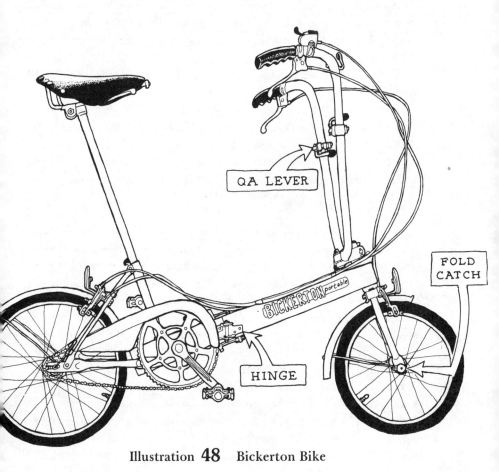

Illustration **48**   Bickerton Bike

electric cement mixer, and I had to take some parts out to his place, up north along the California coast from where I live. Well, the bus could only take me as far as Davenport, but I was ready to go the last five miles on my trusty Bickerton. I mean, five miles would be a cinch, wouldn't it?

I hadn't realized just how hard it is to carry the flywheel of a cement mixer on a bicycle when riding into a 30 mph head-wind, up and down those steep coastal hills. It would have been damned hard on *any* bike. On the Bickerton it was total mad-ness. I wound up folding the handlebars in toward each other so I could balance the flywheel on top of them, holding it there with both hands and a bungee cord. But my knees hit the bars when they were folded in like that. And when the wind gusted, that bike was about as stable as a paper airplane in a typhoon. Well, I made it, and Lou's cement mixer works fine now, but it was quite a while before I tried to do anything adventurous with my Bickerton again.

You can have enough fun just riding it to the train or bus, then riding the bus to work or school or whatever, and using the "Bickey" for all the short errands you need to do on lunch hour or before you catch the bus home. Once you get the hang of setting it up for riding and folding it back into its bag, you can do the whole procedure in about two minutes. If you follow Harry's manual, and tips like the ones below, you can always set it at the same position, the one that's best for you, so it'll be easy and fun to ride.

The first tip is this: Be careful with the aluminum frame. You can't whack it around like you can whack a steel bike frame around. You have to *practice* handling the bike until you can fold and unfold it correctly every time. Don't ever use the bike when you're in so much of a hurry that you can't take the few extra seconds to handle it carefully. Don't lend the bike out to anybody, either, until you have shown them how to treat the thing properly. Make sure they appreciate the light but soft and pliable nature of those aluminum tubes. If you don't take these precautions, parts of the bike will get scratched, bent, warped, and dented so they either don't fit together nicely, or don't stay tight when you do get them together. This can make the bike handle even more like a wet noodle than it does normally. As you follow the directions below, be particularly careful while tightening the parts into position with the Quick Release levers (Harry Bickerton calls them QA or Quick Action levers). Never push a lever so tight that it squishes the aluminum tube inside it.

Unfolding

Grab the bike by the curved tube that's closest to you. This is part of the handlebar, and it's what you hold onto when carrying the folded bike, whether it's in the bag or out of it. Holding that curved bar works better than holding the canvas bag handles because it gives you a firm grip and raises the bike higher off the ground. Hold the bike up in one hand and unsnap the bag snaps with the other so you can push the bag down off the bike. Do it gently, making sure nothing gets snagged on the bag handles or corners. When the bag is off, rest the bike on the wheels, still holding the curved tube so the machine can't tip over or settle forward onto the chain; you don't want to get that chain dirty on the ground if you can help it. Slide the seat and seat post (or seat stem, as Harry calls it) out of their resting place in the folded bike. Stick the post into the seat tube of the frame (the hole will be looking right up at you as you stand over the folded bike) and line up the seat so it's facing in the general direction that will be forward when the bike's unfolded. Tighten the seat post QA lever to keep it there.

Check to see that the right pedal (the one with the sprocket on its crank) is set in the down and forward position (Harry says at 4 o'clock, if you face that crank from its side of the bike), then push the handlebar you've been holding *down* and pull the back end of the bike up by the seat post. There will be a click and the two halves of the bike will swing free of each other if they haven't already. Now hold the back of the bike still with your hand, supporting it by the seat post, and swing the front end of the bike around on the hinge until it's straight.

Set both frame hooks (there's one on top and one on the bottom of the main frame tube) so they touch the flat-sided pole of the frame clamp lever (that's the long lever with the black cap on the end). Turn that lever until it is pointing out to the left side of the bike and forward. Now, if you hold the bike close to straight (watch your fingers; they can get an awful pinch if the frame halves close on them or the hooks catch

Illustration **49**   Unfolding the Bickerton

them) the hooks should both be caught on the flat surfaces of the clamp lever pole. Turn the lever so the hooks get pulled tight on those flats. The frame meshes together firmly and it will stay there until you loosen the lever. It's a lovely bit of engineering. I like the way it makes use of those hardwood plugs inside the frame tube, too.

Loosen the QA levers that bind the handlebars, the stem, and the stem bar together. Swing the bars up, making sure the cables aren't snagged on anything. Swing the bars as far as they will go; they go past straight up before they stop. Lock the handlebar-gripping QA lever so they stay in that position. Then hold the front wheel still between your feet and turn the handlebars *clockwise* until they stop, lined up with the wheel. It may seem odd to move the bars clockwise, because this moves the stem bar toward the back of the bike. The stem sticks out frontward on most bikes, but on the Bickerton it goes backward. Lock the QA lever when that bar is against the stopper, lined up with the front wheel.

Loosen the two QA levers that hold the ends of the handlebars in that ludicrous see-no-evil position, then turn both handlebar ends toward the back of the bike so you can get them in a rideable position without wrapping the cables around the bars. I like to set the bar ends pointing out and back at about a 45-degree angle. Others like to have them pointing farther out. You can raise the bar ends up an inch or so if you're tall, but they're more stable if you leave them shoved all the way down into the lower U tube of the bars.

Take the left pedal out of the place where it's wedged between the rear fender and the bike frame. Look at the threaded end of the spindle that's going to screw into the hold in the left crank. You'll find a little flat metal wrench thingy

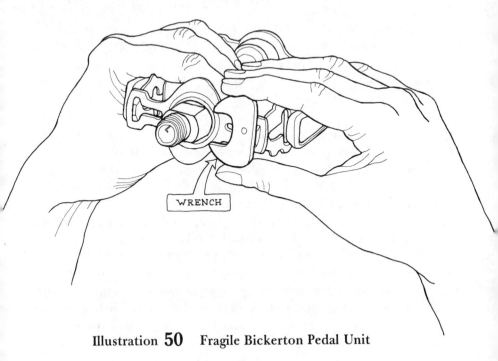

Illustration 50   **Fragile Bickerton Pedal Unit**

that can slide back and forth on the end plate of the pedal. If you turn the spindle so the flat places on it line up with the clever sliding wrench gizmo, you can push the wrench onto those flats and lock the pedal and spindle into a single unit. When it's locked firmly, turn the whole thing COUNTER-CLOCKWISE into the left crank. It has left-handed threads, like all left cranks on bikes. Be very careful as you start threading the pedal in; the aluminum crank can strip out easily if the threads get crossed.

The pedal should screw all the way in, very easily. Tighten it firmly when it's home, but don't put so much oomph into that little wrench gizmo that you warp it. If you plan to leave the bike assembled for a while, use a strong cone wrench or a pedal spanner to do a final tightening of the left pedal, then leave it like that. The bike can be folded up and put in the bag without taking the pedal off. You only need to remove the left pedal if you're going to put the folded bike into a tight space.

The last touch to setting up the Bickerton is to fold up the blue bag it comes in and hang the bag from the two little hooks on the handlebars. This is easier said than done. I've fooled around with Origami a bit, so I don't have too much trouble figuring out how to fold the corners of the bag into the center (they have to overlap in there, and they should be folded all the way to the opposite side, so the white straps are at the outer edge of the bag when you get done) and figuring out which snaps go together in order to hold the whole thing in its final shape.

The two eyelets on the white strap ends are supposed to fit onto the handlebar hooks, but they may not go on without some jockeying around and maybe even a little bending of the hooks. Just go easy on those things, because they are light metal, and I don't know where in the world you'd get replacements other than Harry Bickerton's garage!

Once the bag is in place, it will hold some light luggage, such as a sack lunch or a small notebook and school supplies. You can't put a rear carrier on the Bickerton and fold up the bike as intended, but if you want to carry more stuff and keep up the Bickerton tradition, just get a canvas fold-up backpack to carry things on your back, and keep it folded up in the Bickerton bag or in your own back pocket (see page 10).

Riding the Bike

Take your first ride on your Bickerton in a flat neighborhood, when you've got plenty of time to get the feel of it. You can't be in a hurry to start with. Concentrate on riding with as fluid a cadence as possible. This is easiest on the three-speed model, because you can shift gears as you speed up, and even at top speed the relatively high gear (it feels like about 80 inches or so) makes it possible to pedal with a smooth, easy motion. If you have a single-gear model, you'll find it a bit hard to start off smoothly; the bike will tend to get jerky and unstable at high speed, too. Many riders have found that toe clips help them keep their high rpm pedaling smooth; if it helps you, do it. At low rpm, going uphill, push down hard and smoothly. Do *not* stand up on the pedals, though. You put too much torque on the central frame joint that way. You'll loosen it so much that even tightening up on the adjustable hooks won't keep the bike from creaking and swaying on its hinges.

When you come to short, steep hills, get up a little steam and go up them briskly. If you have gears, shift down before it's necessary, so you never lug and lunge from side to side. Keep your butt glued to the seat, and try to keep your butt *still,* so it doesn't wag the seat post back and forth like a flagpole in an earthquake. Don't pull back on the handlebars, either; no matter how tight you set the QA lever, you can twist those bars back into your lap if you yank too hard on them.

If you can't make it all the way to the top of a hill at a smooth, brisk pace, stop and walk the rest of the way. With practice, you'll find that you can take the light machine up surprisingly steep grades without having to get off; on your first rides, though, don't strain the machine or yourself.

Make sure the tires are adequately inflated (80 pounds rear, 60 pounds front) so the bike makes firm contact with the pavement. Don't go over curbs or big rocks; the shock can ruin the frame or the fenders, even if the tires are hard. Don't do any weaving or stunt riding on a Bickerton, either. These activities will loosen the joints and fatigue the aluminum. The noodly feel of the bike makes it tempting, I know, but don't push the little critter farther than it can go.

When riding in traffic, you'll love the way the bike can start, stop, and turn so quickly. For optimum visibility, you may want to raise the handlebars and lower the seat so you can sit straight and look around with ease. I've found the leaning-forward position plenty convenient, but those of you who are more used to riding a sit-up bike may like the raised-bar position better.

Be prepared for lots of laughter, no matter how you set the bike up. People usually think you've taken a kid's bike and rigged it up with seat and handlebar extensions. You must admit, you *do* look pretty strange when riding on the Bickerton. To me, the enjoyment I give pedestrians is just fine, and the fact that car drivers notice a Bickerton more than a regular bike is a big plus for it. I don't give a hoot if they're laughing at me, as long as they see me and are less likely to run me down. Remember the old rap about eye contact (see page 27)? A Bickerton seems to be a very effective tool for establishing eye contact.

Keep the Bickerton away from dirt roads, trails, and other dusty or muddy situations. The thing isn't made for rough treatment, and if the sliding parts get dirty at the joints they will be much harder to fold and unfold. They will also wear out until they don't fit together at all. The chain, by the way, is nickel-plated, so you don't have to oil it much. Graphite lubricants, molybdenum disulphide, or even WD-40 spray lube will do. Wipe off any extra lubricant, so the chain doesn't get you and the bag dirty as you handle the bike. As long as you don't leave the bike out in the rain or ride it around on dusty roads the chain will hold its light lubrication for many weeks.

Sometimes, after a particularly steep hill-climb, or after a heavy person has been riding the Bickerton hard, you'll hear the main frame joint squeak and creak. Don't be alarmed at this; you can ride for days with a squeaky frame joint and it won't break. But it's not good for the frame, and the longer you leave it loose and wobbly, the harder it will be to get it tight again. The parts can get worn and distorted to the point where you have to replace them, and that's a hard thing to do with a Bickerton. Few shops carry spares.

To tighten up your squeaky frame joint, first loosen the frame hooks by turning the locking lever out to the side of the frame, thus unlocking the joint. Take two open end wrenches in hand (a crescent and a 13 mm open-end wrench will do fine) and loosen up the two nuts on one of the hooks. Tighten the nut that's on the straight end of the hook while holding the hook still so it can't twist around cockeyed. Tighten the end nut only one-sixth of a turn at a time. That means moving one of the flat sides of the nut to the position of the adjacent flat. It doesn't take much to tighten the frame joint up considerably, and you don't want the thing so tight that you bend the metal every time you lock the joint up.

When you have tightened the nut a sixth of a turn, loosen the two nuts on the other hook and tighten the end nut up on that hook by the same amount you tightened the first one. Then put the hooks around the locking lever and lock the lever tight. It should be a little hard to lock the lever, but not so hard that you can't do it with the fingers of one hand. If the hooks are still loose, tighten up the end nuts on them another sixth of a turn or so, and make sure the hooks stay straight on the lever pole as you do it. If you can't keep them from twisting, hold the locknut on the hook with your second wrench as you tighten the end nut. When you've got the hooks set at the right tightness, and equally tight with each other, hold the end nut still with one wrench and tighten the lock nut *hard* against the post that holds the hook. It has to be tight so the hook won't twist around and miss the lever, or work itself loose as you are riding.

Folding Up the Bickerton

Harry's quaint instructions tell you to reverse the unfolding procedure to get the Bickerton back in the bag. If only it were that simple. Start by loosening all the handlebar QA levers. Fold the bar ends in to the center, making sure the RIGHT handlebar grip is in FRONT (toward the front end of the bike) of the left handlebar grip. Tighten the QA levers just a little so the bar ends won't fall out, then turn the bars so they fold down on the right side of the front wheel, as shown in Illustration 49. Push them down snug against the wheel, then tighten the two stem QA levers a bit so the bars can't get loose. Make sure the right-hand pedal is in the 4 o'clock position, pointing down and forward, as shown in Illustration 49.

Loosen the frame joint locking lever and fold the bike in half. Turn both the hooks and the lever so they're in line with the frame tube, out of your way as you swing the front half of the bike back to mesh with the back half. Once the bike's folded, try to keep the chain up off the ground, especially if the ground is dusty. Tip the folded bike up on its front wheel, then push on the rear wheel (grab it by the hub for a firm push) and lock the two ends of the bike together by means of the little bent washer that's on the front axle. Harry Bickerton calls this washer the fold catch, but it's just a bent washer, and it won't work unless the bike is folded up just right.

There are various things that may make it impossible for you to get that washer hooked on the dropout of the rear wheel. The three-speed indicator chain may be hitting the front wheel spokes, or the wheels may not be in line with each other (the front wheel may be steering to one side or the other), or the handlebar ends may not be folded against the front wheel snugly, or one of the handlebar end QA levers may be pushing against the rear wheel. Look down between the wheels as you try to push the rear wheel in against the front one. When you feel something blocking your progress, look all around in that tangle of machinery until you find out what is doing the blocking. On my bike the culprit is usually one of the handlebar QA levers. I loosen or tighten it until it clears the rear wheel, then the whole thing slips together and stays put beautifully. I just hope you can find the blockage if you have any trouble getting your Bickerton to stay folded. It's a real pain to load and unload a Bickerton if it keeps unfolding on you.

All you have to do after folding and "catching" the frame is to undo the seat post QA lever, slide the seat post out of the frame, then slip it along the top of the chain guard, starting at the rounded front end of the guard. The post fits between the rear fender brace and the wheel, and you slide the seat all the way in until it nestles into the machinery, point up. You can slip a loop of brake and/or gear cable around the back of the seat to hold it there.

The bike may be put into the bag just as it is now, or you can take the left pedal off if you want to make it an easier fit and a narrower package when you're finished. The left pedal makes a big lump on one side of the bag if you leave it in place, and it makes the thing harder to pack into a small place, like under your seat on a bus, train, or airplane. To take the pedal off, turn it to the right position so you can slide the flat wrench gizmo into place, then unscrew the spindle CLOCKWISE to remove it from the crank. Make sure you take it straight out of the crank so it doesn't damage those tender aluminum threads in there. Stick the end of the spindle in the hole in the frame behind the tube; if you want to make sure it stays put, wedge it between the fender and the seat tube as you push the spindle into that hole.

Putting the folded bike into the bag is one of those operations that calls for six or eight hands, even though there's only room for two people to work on it. I've found it easiest to do the job by myself, concentrating on getting the thing lined up right at the start, so it doesn't put up too much of a fight as the bag goes around it.

Make sure the bike is completely folded and the fold catch is caught. See that the locking lever and the hooks at the frame joint are all folded back out of the way. They snag on the bag if they're not. Then put the bag down on its bottom, unsnap the

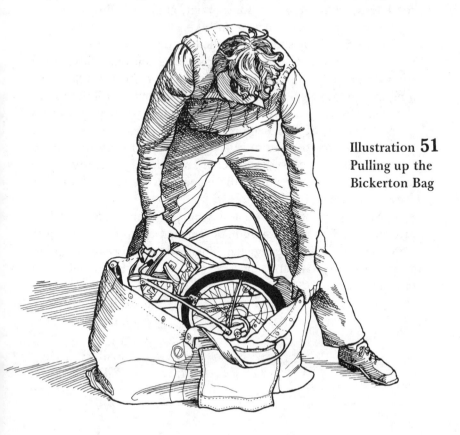

Illustration 51
Pulling up the
Bickerton Bag

snaps, and furl the sides down and away from the center, so you can see the inside of the bottom of the bag. Lift the bike by the curve of the handlebar that's right at the top, and settle it down on the bottom of the bag. Take one end of the bag and pull it up around the right pedal and the frame joint. I know, I know—the pedal tends to get caught and spin backward, the fold catch tends to come undone, and the whole bike conspires to swing open, pinch your fingers, knock your shins, and make you look ridiculous to any bystanders. This is why it's important to practice handling the bike before you start using it out in public. If you're rushing for a bus, and you blow something as you're trying to stuff the bike into the bag, it will embarrass and harry you, and you might lose your temper and treat those delicate aluminum tubes with less respect than they deserve. If one of them gets ruined, you'll look even more ridiculous trying to ride your Bickerton with only half its parts put together. So practice the bag trick, the reverse Houdini act, and get it down perfect, to save your pride as well as your bike.

Once you have smoothly pulled up one end of the bag over the folded end of the bike, pull the other end of the bag over the wheels and seat. The canvas will roll on the wheels, and as long as it doesn't sneak under the rear fender, you'll soon have the bag covering the folded bike completely. Snap the snaps near the ends of the bag, and you can pick up the whole business and step onto your bus, plane, boat, or whatever. Carry the thing by that curved handlebar tube that's so handy there, and you'll put less strain on the bag and parts of the bike that press against it.

After you have done the whole folding and unfolding procedure a few times, you'll be amazed at how you can just flow through it like a magician. Then, when you're really quick at it, those bystanders who are so ready to laugh will gape in wonderment.

Chapter 14
Adding a Mini-motor to Your Bicycle

MOST GAS engines are a bother, but there are a few good small motors you can use on your bicycle to travel long distances. The better motors can get as much as 250 miles per gallon, which is way more efficient than any car or motorcycle. If you ride a lot, like I do, you may not want to have a motor anywhere near your favorite bike. But if you can use a motor on a second bike, like a heavy-duty ten-speed or a sturdy old three-speed, it will be much better than using a car on trips that are too long for normal cycling. I mean, rather than trying to get a more efficient car at a cost of several thousand dollars, why not try a super-efficient bike motor for a couple hundred?

There are two basic places a motor can be added to a bike; on the front wheel, or on the rear wheel. In Japan there are motors that hang under the bottom bracket, but these are not allowed in the U.S. Of the two available options, the recognized leader of front-wheel motors is the Bike Bug, made by AquaBug International (see Addresses).

The Bike Bug uses principles that have been employed on the French Solex Moped for decades, but the Bike Bug is a much more advanced, efficient, and solid motor, and it also has the advantage of being removable. There is nothing harder than pedaling a Solex around with a motor that's kaput. While the Bike Bug is a great little motor, and very quiet too, it does have certain elements you have to be careful about.

The friction roller that turns your bike wheel is soft; it wears down to match the shape of your front tire for the best possible traction. If you don't use the motor correctly, or if you don't keep it adjusted so it has a firm contact with the front wheel, it's easy to wear out the friction roller more in one place than another, so it runs unevenly and sends nasty vibrations shuddering through the bike's frame and yours as well. These can be avoided if you follow the mounting and adjustment instructions below, and make sure you always engage and disengage the friction roller briskly, so it starts and stops without skidding against the front tire.

Even if the friction roller does get bumpy or worn out, you can replace it for a reasonable price, so this one basic weakness of the Bike Bug does not detract too much from its value. It is my first choice for a motor to put on a bike. It is also sold under several other names, in bike and moped shops, so if you find a motor that looks just like the one in Illustration 52, but has another name or no name on it, don't worry. It's just a Bike Bug with another marketing channel.

There is another motor you can put on the back of your bike, the Bike Machine, by K and S Industries. It appears to be a sturdy, simple unit of basically sound design, but it was not available at press time, and even when it comes out, it may not be as simple to use or as reliable as the Bike Bug, for a few reasons that I can see just by looking at the photos and literature about it. It has a pull-start and a centrifugal clutch, so the motor can keep running when you come to a stop, even though

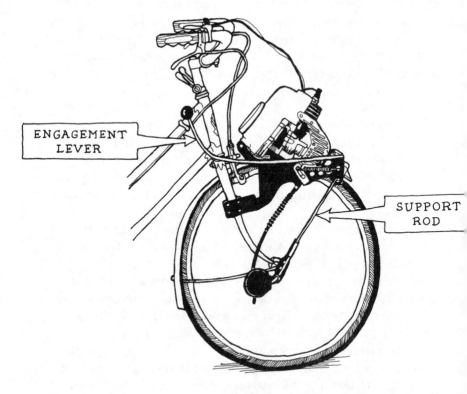

ENGAGEMENT
LEVER

SUPPORT
ROD

Illustration 52   Bike Bug Motor

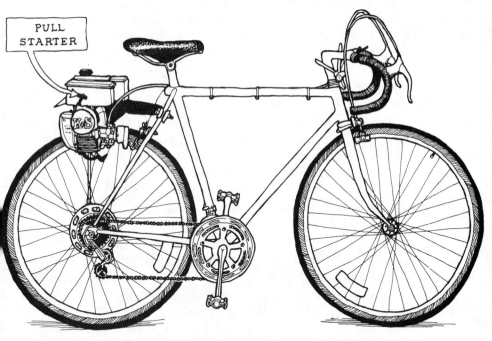

PULL
STARTER

Illustration **53** **Rear-Mounted Motor**

you don't pull it up off the wheel. That's a nice idea, but it
means you have to pull-start the thing, rather than just putting
it on the wheel and letting the bike's motion start it. Also, pull-
starters and centrifugal clutches can give you a lot of trouble.
Even on the best small engines, they tend to go awry after
heavy use. The other things that bother me about the Bike
Machine are the way it is mounted to the bike frame and the
fact that it's hard to disengage and turn off while you're riding.
The clamp that holds the motor to the bike's seat stays is a
simple one-bolt unit that reminds me of the cheapest racks and
child seats. It doesn't even have any rubber padding that I can
see, so it is bound to either squish the seat stays if you tighten it
too hard, or work loose and let the motor down on the bike's
brakes if you don't tighten it enough. And it is certain to deliver
a lot of vibration to the bike frame no matter how you tighten
it. If the clamp is not improved when the motor comes onto the
market, you should improve it yourself. Either figure out some
way to attach the connecting bar to your frame using the Blackburn stay clamps (see Illustration 20), or at least use a strong
support (as in Illustration 5) to shore the thing up.

Although I like the idea of having the motor behind you so you don't have to look at it, you should have some way of disengaging the motor or at least turning it off without getting off the bike and going back there to look after it. I mean, what if the little rascal gets stuck in high throttle? The motor should have a convenient kill-switch, at least. The Bike Bug has an automatic shut-off that kills the engine immediately if you slam on the brakes, and it also has a kill-switch incorporated into the throttle lever.

The Bike Machine does look like a basically sound unit, though. And if the makers improve on the design (they claim it is being improved at press time), it will be a viable alternative, especially if you want to avoid having extra weight on the front of your bike, or if you want to have a basket up there. The instructions for the mounting and use of a bike motor below apply mainly to the Bike Bug, but if you get a Bike Machine you can use much of the information, keeping in mind the obvious differences in design between the two motors.

Setting Bike Up for a Bike Bug

You can put the Bike Bug on almost any bike, even one with a front fender, but the machine will work best and last longest if you have a good, sturdy bike with wheels that are at least 26 inches in diameter and at least an inch wide. To improve the efficiency of the motor's traction, get a tire for your bike that has a wide, flat-topped profile. This sort of tire is *not* the best for sporty riding (see Illustration 2). But it will give the motor's friction wheel the widest, strongest surface possible to roll on, especially if you keep it inflated to the correct pressure at all times. If you are going to use the bike with and without the motor (it's easy to put on and take off, as you'll see) you may want to get a spare front wheel for your bike, one that is strong and that has a wide tire on it. You can switch to your narrow, ridged tire and light wheel for motorless riding. Wheels with quick-release levers will make the switch a snap.

To keep the vibration of the motor and bike to an absolute minimum, check the headset and front wheel bearings on your bike to make sure they are not loose and rattly. The motor's weight requires steering that works just right, too, so don't make the headset either too loose *or* too tight. If you are unsure of the procedure for adjusting those bearings, see a good bike manual like *Anybody's Bike Book* and get them set perfectly. Make sure your brakes are good, too. You may need them to work quickly and effectively, to stop the motor as well as the bike.

To attach the motor, just follow the fine instructions included with it. I will summarize them here, in case you lose them, or get the motor secondhand. Unpack the motor, the support rod, the throttle lever/kill switch, and the exhaust system and make sure they are all in good condition. Park your bike where it won't roll away or turn over. If you have a shop stand or a Flickstand, use it to keep the bike still while you work on it. You don't want the motor to roll down the front wheel of the bike and take a bounce off the floor. Loosen the fork clamps so you can slip them onto your forks.

Lift the motor into the position shown in Illustration 52, making sure the fork clamps settle around the forks nicely. The fit will be tighter on some forks than others, but when you tighten all of the bolts and nuts it will be plenty strong, even if your forks have an unusual shape. Make sure, as you tighten the bolts and nuts, that the motor stays squarely above the front wheel, so it will ride level and its friction roller will rest evenly on the front tire. Tighten the bolts a little on one side, then a little on the other side, so you can keep things even all around as you go.

Remove the right axle nut or quick-release cone from your front wheel and put the bracket for the muffler and support rod on the end of the axle. Put the nut or QR cone back on and tighten it very firmly, making sure the wheel is still centered between the brake pads and forks, and the bracket is aimed right, so the rod slips up and down in it easily. Adjust the wingnut on the support rod so it lifts the engine, raising the friction roller ¼-inch above the fully inflated tire when the clutch or engagement lever is pushed down. Push the exhaust tube onto the metal pipe that sticks down from the bottom of the engine and secure both ends of the tube with the little tightening rings.

Attach the throttle lever/kill switch to your handlebars, either near the right end, or, if you have a three-speed switch there, near the left end. Set it at such an angle that you can reach it easily with your thumb as you ride, so you can change your speed conveniently or turn the thing off quickly. As the Bike Bug people are proud to point out, you don't have to touch the lever if you're stopping suddenly. The automatic cut-off switch in the engine will turn it off for you. But it's still nice to have the control close at hand.

To fill the fuel tank with gas and oil, use a large can of fuel that has already been mixed to the proper ratio. Some motors take 25 parts gas to 1 part oil, and others take a 50 to 1 ratio. Make *sure* you know which your engine needs. You can use the mix-in-the-tank method, carefully measuring the correct amounts of gas and oil, but this works accurately only when the tank is empty.

Riding with a Bike Bug

Before you start the motor, first push the clutch or engagement lever down so the friction roller is clear of the front tire. Set the throttle at idle, then pedal the bike in a low gear until it is going about five miles an hour, just fast enough so you don't have any trouble balancing. Then lift the engagement lever crisply so the friction roller drops onto the bike wheel and starts turning immediately. If you raise the lever slowly, the compression of the engine may hold the roller still, so it skids on the tire and rapidly wears into an uneven, vibrating mess. When the roller turns smoothly, on the other hand, the motor will start right up. The starting performance of the Bike Bug is excellent, so you don't have to worry about whether the motor will actually turn over. You'll feel the difference when it starts to pull you, adjust the throttle at this time, to go whatever speed you want. In town, you have to keep the speed way down until you are completely used to driving on a moped with a thumb-controlled throttle. It is not like a car and it is not like a motorcycle with a twist-grip throttle. Practice at low speeds, where there is little traffic, before you venture out into the congested thoroughfares, where you need to pick up and lose speed quickly. It *is* a thrill to start pedaling along, then feel that strong, quiet little motor take over and zoom you up to 20 miles per hour or so, but don't let the thrill go to your head. Keep your eyes on traffic, not on the engine.

If you feel vibration coming from the motor, stop and find out what the trouble is. It will only get worse if you let it go on shaking. The problem will probably be that the mounting clamps are loose, or the friction roller is getting worn unevenly. Replace the roller or tighten the bolts, so you can get humming along without any shake-and-jiggle.

When you come to a stop sign, slow down almost to a complete stop by lowering the throttle and braking, then pedal through the intersection and raise the throttle to pick up speed again. If you have to come to a complete stop to wait for traffic, push the engagement or clutch lever down before you come to the stop, so the motor can run at idle until you get going again. When you pick up a little speed (to about 5 mph) after waiting until traffic clears, pull the lever up, let the motor begin to pull you, then increase the throttle until you get going at the cruising speed that's comfortable for you. Always engage and disengage the friction roller crisply, at low speed, so it doesn't skid on the tire and get a flat spot worn into it.

Don't take corners too fast. When you're just getting used to the machine, slow down way before you think it's necessary so you don't have to try to brake and throttle down in the middle of the turn. Keep enough speed so you can balance easily (the bike will be tippy if you only go two or three miles per hour), but take the turns with caution until you are in tune with the moped's handling characteristics. The weight and power on the front wheel make it seem tricky at first, but once you are used to the feeling you'll be able to lean and glide through curves with the greatest of ease.

To make your trips as simple and relaxed as possible, pick routes where you don't have to do lots of stop-and-go driving. This will save wear on the friction roller as well as your nerves. The gasoline engine does its best work when it is cruising along at an even rpm, making the maximum mileage out of each thimbleful of gasoline used. You'll be astounded at how far you can go when you use the thing right.

Maintenance

Like any gasoline engine, the Bike Bug must be looked after. Because it's so simple, there really aren't many things to keep up with, but you should check the spark plug at least three times a year, or if you ever have trouble getting the motor started. If the plug is all black and gunky, or if the points are worn and burnt away, replace the plug and make SURE you use the fuel mixture that is correct. Too much or too little oil in the gas can wreck the plug and hurt the engine eventually, too. If you replace the plug, get the new one from a reputable moped or small engine shop, and make doubly sure it is the exact same plug as the original. Many mechanics say that any old plug will do, but I would beg to differ. There is only one best spark plug for any engine, and that is the one the manufacturer recommends for that engine. If you have trouble finding a replacement, write or call the manufacturer (see Addresses) who will help you find one, or mail one to you directly. It's worth the trouble on a simple engine like a Bike Bug, because it's the only thing that needs to be replaced normally, and it makes a big difference in performance.

Take the air cleaner apart and clean the element every spring and every fall, or more often if you ride on dusty or smoggy roads a lot. All you have to do is remove the screws, take the cover off, and pull the element out. Soak it in a solvent, brush and wipe the junk off, then put a few drops of oil on the element and work it around like a sponge before you put it back in the engine.

Check the roller every thousand miles or so, or look at it closely if the motor starts to shake on the bike. The roller is designed to wear quickly at first so it will conform to the shape of your tire. Then it will wear more slowly, especially if you treat it nicely. After the first break-in period, you'll have to lower the setting of the support rod (turn the wingnut counterclockwise) so the surface of the worn roller will be within a quarter-inch of the tire again. As the roller continues to wear slowly, you'll have to adjust that support every month or so in order to keep the roller low enough so it never slips on the tire. If you have a wide, flat-topped tire, it will take longer to wear down to the point that it needs adjustment.

Finally the roller will wear down so much that there isn't much of the black tread left on it. At this point, order a new roller from AquaBug International. It costs about eight percent of the price of the whole motor, which isn't much when you consider how much you have to pay for most essential bike parts such as cranks and gear changers.

As a final word on the Bike Bug, I must say that I don't own one. The motor is impressive, and I can see lots of situations in which it will make sense to have one in these gas-starved days. But for right now, I'm going to get by with a bike for all short trips and even some long ones, while using mass transit to do longer trips by myself, and using our small station wagon to take the family on long outings. The day may soon come when it will be hard to get enough gas for any long trips in a private automobile. When that day comes, I hope the Bike Bug will still be around, because it will fill a big gap.

Postscript

My love affair with bikes doesn't end here.
I'll love cycling until I can't do it anymore,
probably longer. But in any long affair,
things change. I'll learn new things to do
with bikes, and new bikes will come along
that teach me new ways to enjoy cycling.
If you like cycling too, you can help the
whole romance along if you ever learn something about bikes I haven't written about,
or something that I haven't covered well
enough. Just send your idea or improvement
to me, care of the publisher, and we'll put
it in the next edition, so everybody can
join in, making even better use of that most
useful and lovable of all machines,
The Bicycle.

Addresses

Catalogues

Bikecology
(10-Speed parts, frames, cycle clothing)
P.O. Box 1880
Santa Monica, CA 90406

Cycling Handbook (racing and
touring bikes, parts, tools)
Flying Dutchman
P.O. Box 20352
Denver, CO 80220

Early Winters (camping gear,
Super rain booties)
110 Prefontaine Place South
Seattle, WA 98104

Cycl-ology (parts for *all* types of bikes)
Cycle Goods
2735 Hennepin Avenue South
Minneapolis, MN 55408

Bike Warehouse (touring and tandem
frames and parts)
P.O. Box 290
New Middleton, OH 44442

Magazines

BICYCLING
33 East Minor Street
Emmaus, PA 18049

BIKE WORLD
1400 Stierlin Road
Mountain View, CA 94043

Touring Organizations

American Youth Hostel
A.Y.H. National Headquarters
Delaplane, VA 22025

OR

See Regional Office of A.Y.H.
in nearest large city.

Snow and Ice Tire Studs

I. P. Limhike
206 West Works
Sheridan, NY 82801

Portable Bicycles

Harry Bickerton
The Old Engineer's House
Terwin Water
Welwyn, Herts, England

Hub and Axle Bicycle Works
(Pocket Bike)
83 Eldredge Street
Newton, MA 02158

Supine Bicycles

Martin-Dean Easy-racer
2891 Freedom Blvd.
Watsonville, CA 95076

Manuped Inc.
1557 McKinley Street
Eugene, OR 97402

Rearview Mirrors

Bikecology and Bike Warehouse
(see *Catalogues*)

Michael Benthin
21 Pleasant View Drive
Strasbourg, PA 17579

Bicycle Mini-Motors

Rear mounted motor:
K and S Industries
P.O. Box 612
Fort Worth, TX 76101

Front Wheel "Bike Bug" or
Spitz Motor:
Inside Edge
624 Glen Street
Glen Falls, NY 12801

OR

Aqua-Bug International
100 Merrick Road
Rockville Centre, NY 11570

Bicycle Trucks

Cycle Goods (see Cycl-ology
under *Catalogues*)

Worksman Bicycles
94–15 100th Street
Ozone Park, NY 11416